CROSSCURRENTS AND CONFLUENCES: ECHOES OF RELIGION IN TWENTIETH-CENTURY FICTION

Eamon Maher

VERITAS

First published 2000 by
Veritas Publications
7/8 Lower Abbey Street
Dublin 1

Copyright © Eamon Maher, 2000

All rights reserved. No part of any contribution to this volume may be
reproduced, stored in a retrieval system, or transmitted, in any form or by
any means, electronic, mechanical, photocopying, recording, or otherwise without the prior permission of the copyright holder.

ISBN 1 85390 454 6

British Library Cataloguing
in Publication Data.
A catalogue record for
this book is available
from the British Library.

Cover design by Barbara Croatto
Printed in the Republic of Ireland by Betaprint Ltd, Dublin

To Dad, my first reader and best critic.

ACKNOWLEDGEMENTS

The author would like to thank the following journals for granting permission to reproduce material: *The Month, Doctrine & Life, The Irish Theological Quarterly,* and *Studies.*

Thanks also to Síne Quinn, whose enthusiasm for the project was apparent from the outset and whose editing has been essential in ensuring the quality of the finished product; to Barbara Croatto for the cover design, and to Fr Nivard Kinsella, whose insights and advice with the initial manuscript are much appreciated.

CONTENTS

FOREWORD

It has been said, without overmuch exaggeration, that for several generations the cultural capital of the Irish writer/intellectual was Paris. Oscar Wilde and George Moore were at least half-French by culture, Yeats drew on French symbolism, Edith Somerville studied art there, Synge lived there for a period and Joyce felt totally at home in Paris and, indeed, encountered more recognition and intellectual fellowship in France than he did in England. And for Irish painters, Paris was the art capital of the world, where the most advanced paintings might be viewed and the latest visual techniques mastered at the various art colleges and academies.

More recently, Beckett and Behan were both Francophiles, while Seán O'Faoláin drew heavily on French influences and attitudes for both his fiction and his polemical writings. During the thirties and forties, French neo-Thomism (personified by Jacques Maritain) had a considerable impact on Irish Catholic intellectuals, and slightly later Conor Cruise O'Brien's critical study, *Maria Cross,* set up spreading ripples (in those days, his perceptive writings on contemporary French literature were generally published under the pseudonym of Donat O'Donnell). Certain Irish poets of the same era, notably Denis Devlin and Brian Coffey, can hardly be understood without the background of this intellectual French Catholicism, which almost inevitably was suspect to many of the Irish clergy.

France, of course, was a libertarian republic and as such, her political system was more congenial to many Irish people than that of monarchist Britain. This political link goes back centuries in history, as is well known. However, it was not primarily political affinities that drew so many Irish writers to France, or at least to its contemporary culture and thought. One of the attractions was certainly the religious aspect, even if France was no longer a predominantly Catholic country. The tensions, dark areas and occasional illuminations of the Catholic conscience continued to haunt French writing even when the average French person had long ceased attending Mass. A thinking, sentient Irish person could identify with this emotional and spiritual world of guilt and repentance, and even alienation, in a way he or she could not do so with contemporary English writing, give or take a few notable exceptions. And without the idiocies of Irish censorship, French novelists could move in several fields (including the sexual one) which were largely denied to their Irish counterparts.

Eamon Maher has chosen five French and five Irish novelists who belong, very broadly speaking, to the period I have mentioned. Not all of them have necessarily worn well, if considered purely as artists – Mauriac, a Nobel Prize winner, no longer seems to me the commanding figure he once was, and Bernanos, too, is rather out of fashion. Camus, one of the intellectual heroes of existentialism, is a contrasting figure since he typifies the angst and 'tragic humanism' which was a widespread reaction among the post-war intelligentsia to the horrors of the Holocaust and the inhumanity of the Nagasaki and Hiroshima bombings. Western people – and not only he – seemed to be living in the mushroom-shaped shadow of the atomic bomb.

Julien Green does not fit into any category except his own, since he was Franco-American and an anguished homosexual who never could come to terms with his own sexuality. I think Eamon Maher is quite right to point out his isolated position as a writer in France, and perhaps he has more in common intellectually with the Northern European Protestant

Kierkegaard than with his French contemporaries. Yet allowing for this, can he not be linked also with a tradition that stems from Pascal and the Jansenists of Port Royal, who were (very generally speaking) to Post-Reformation Catholicism what Calvin (also a Frenchman) was to Lutheranism? Green had a formidable intelligence which seems to stand curiously apart from and outside the epoch he lived through, and his sensibility may in some respects be closer to us today than it was forty years ago.

Of the Irish writers he discusses, John Broderick was a personal friend of mine, while I met Kate O'Brien and Brian Moore on a few occasions, but was never remotely intimate with either. Kate O'Brien is particularly interesting, as a woman with an innately Catholic sensibility who was repelled by many aspects of Irish life and religion; Moore is yet another case of a writer more valued abroad (particularly in America) than at home. Taken overall, Eamon Maher's choices are independent-minded, his discussion of them is clear and thoughtful, and his critical judgements are – well, judicious. For those who do not know all these writers in the original, he provides a useful introduction, and for those who have read at least some of them, he gives the stimulus to re-read and reconsider.

Brian Fallon

INTRODUCTION

I have long been fascinated with the links between religion and literature. In my estimation, the truly great writers have a pronounced spiritual quality that raises them above the ordinary. They are the ones who succeed in generating a sense of the poetic, of the invisible, which is more real than the visible, of the rare beauty that is contained in what at first appears merely mundane, or even ugly, to the untutored eye. So when my university studies brought me into contact with some of the main French writers of the twentieth century, I was intrigued with how their experience and treatment of religion differed from that of Irish writers of the same period. Why were Irish writers so hung up on sex, I asked myself, which they tended to associate invariably with sin? Was it as a result of the influence of Jansenism, introduced to this country mainly by Irish priests trained in France during Penal times?[1] I found among some Irish writers an acquaintance with, and admiration for, French literature. While noting similarities, it was impossible to avoid the reality that the two literary traditions diverged through the vagaries of history and the differing cultures pertaining in each case. France had long been a cultural icon before Ireland ever began to be recognised as a country (and not just another British colony) renowned for its writers. Joyce and Beckett chose France as their preferred place of exile, finding Ireland a backward and anti-cultural community. Censorship, ostracism and emigration steadily became the norm for Irish artists from the early decades of the twentieth century, prompting the comment from Beckett that the Irish nation never 'gave a fart in its corduroys for any form of art whatever before the Union or after'.[2] Such a verdict ignores both Irish history and Ireland's distorted culture – in brief, it is a somewhat simplistic assessment.

Our writers became increasingly isolated and felt threatened in a State that was only given international recognition in 1921 and that struggled with internal discord for years after the 1922 Civil War. The new leaders were concerned with creating an Irish identity that would distinguish us from the English. That leaders like Éamon de Valera associated Irishness with a strong rural community, with the Gaelic language and the majority religion, Catholicism, should not surprise us. Neither should it shock that the Irish Catholic Church played an influential role in establishing and consolidating a type of xenophobic fear of Protestantism that dated back to on the Famine period. Catholic priests and bishops had suffered persecution and injustice during British occupation and needed reassurance from an Irish suffrage. They thus sought to ensure that the Constitution of the Irish Republic would enshrine the dominant position of Catholicism as the faith of the Irish people. There is but a small step from being repressed to being triumphalist and this was what took place in Ireland in the early years after Independence, in the twenties, thirties and forties.

An opportunity to demonstrate to the world the loyalty of the Irish people to their Catholic faith and to Rome was provided by the Eucharistic Congress, which was held in Dublin in June 1932. It should be noted that Fianna Fáil (who had just come to power) did not always enjoy good relations with the Catholic Church since the time of the Civil War, as many of their supporters had been excommunicated. That said, de Valera was too astute a politician to allow the past to interfere with the present. A committed Catholic, even if not outwardly pious, he saw the excitement of the people in the run-up to the Congress and was not going to do anything to dampen what was a genuine outpouring of faith. Dermot Keogh captures the significance of the event in the following manner:

> The Eucharistic Congress brought to Dublin representatives from all over the Catholic world. The power of the Irish in the Catholic Church was manifest. More importantly, the Irish Catholic diaspora reassembled to celebrate the 'resurrection': the victory of the two halves of the one struggle – Catholic emancipation and national independence. Thus, an editorial in *The Irish Press* stated: 'The union of the Christian ideal and the national endeavour has been manifested in every great moment of our history.' The Eucharistic Congress in Dublin was not simply a religious celebration. It was a manifestation of Irish Catholic nationalism.[3]

In the emerging State that was the Irish Republic in 1932, it is not difficult to see how religion and nationalism became so inextricably linked. We will see in the chapters on the Irish novelists how those writers who dared to treat in a disparaging manner of matters that were seen as the domain of the Church, were to become alienated and marginalised. Any novels with titles, jacket-designs or illustrations that might suggest a lewd content were forwarded to the Censorship of Publications Board. Most Irish writers suffered the indignity of having at least one of their novels banned. Things even got to the ludicrous stage that not being banned by the Censorship Board was considered something of a slight. The conflict between writers and the leaders of the Catholic Church who were, rightly or wrongly, considered to have a major say in what books were banned, was quite pronounced up until the 1970s, when censorship became more relaxed. As society became more and more secular due to internationally accepted standards of behaviour, censorship became meaningless. TV, films and magazines helped to break down the protective barriers.

The same type of scenario was not evident in twentieth-century France. Ever since the French Revolution, the power of the Catholic Church had been swept away and there was a strong tradition of independent thinking on all issues (sexual, political, moral, religious) among intellectuals. Diatribes against the Church were commonplace in France as early as the sixteenth century (Rabelais' satires, for example, were scathing of malpractice within the Church), while Enlightenment thinkers such as Montesquieu and Voltaire fostered a strong anti-clerical attitude among generations of French people. There was a momentary and important Catholic Revival at the end of the nineteenth and the beginning of the twentieth century, but this did not challenge the advent of systems of thought such as existentialism, structuralism and Marxism, all of which relegated the spiritual to the margins. The level of religious practice among French Catholics fell alarmingly in the first half of the century, partly as a result of increased urbanisation (a factor that also affected religious practice in Ireland), but probably more because the Church increasingly spoke a language that was outdated and largely incomprehensible in the opinion of many people. Jean Sulivan wrote in the 1960s:

> The priests of my youth tended to preach about laws and obligations. In this way, they had succeeded in transforming Christianity into something approaching a natural religion. In their eyes the rural order in which the Church still played a dominant role was an expression of the divine will. They had forgotten about freedom, without which there is no real faith.[4]

There are some obvious parallels between the themes that priests in France and Ireland preached about, if the above quote is an accurate summary of what was emphasised by priests in Sulivan's youth in Brittany. Religion cannot productively be reduced to laws and obligations. The Catholic Church has often fallen into the trap of attempting to provide clear boundaries where none exists, to stress certainty where uncertainty is the reality. Laying down the law, telling people to 'offer up' their suffering, to do this, not do that, will work when you're dealing with black-and-white situations and simple minds, but the grey areas are what cause most difficulties. Accepting your sinfulness is an essential part on the path to salvation, loving yourself in spite of all your faults and failings. The French possessed more analytical minds than the Irish, in part as a result of their philosophical training. They were less likely to accept without question ex-cathedra statements on issues such as sin and grace, good and evil. The average Irish person had never been encouraged or trained to question priests, which often led to the latter assuming that what they said was always correct. An illustration of this is provided by Tony Flannery's account of his experience of the priesthood:

> Generations of deference by the people to him and his predecessors in the clergy, of acceptance of the priest's power over them, a belief that the priest knew best what was good for the people, had contributed to making priests into what they too often became: men who exercised power over their people, rather than being what they were ordained to be, the servants of the people.[5]

The Church in Ireland is probably still suffering from the excesses of the abuse of power by some Irish clergy in the first half of the century. But the recent sexual scandals involving high-profile priests and bishops, and the harrowing TV documentaries revealing what went on in the industrial schools and orphanages up to very recently, have served to cause many sincere Irish Catholics to question their continued membership of the institutional Church and to reinforce others in their opposition to it. But the actions of a minority shouldn't taint the great work done by Irish priests, Christian Brothers and nuns in educating generations of young Irish people and providing care for the underprivileged when the State could not, or did not, provide such necessities. Sure there were many abuses, but corporal punishment and strict discipline were not simply the domain of the religious – plenty of lay people were as bad, and worse, perpetrators of violence and abuse. In Ireland today, the wheel has come full circle and the Church has been relegated to a minority concern for the majority of people, who tend to make up their own minds about what constitutes proper behaviour. Freedom has become the norm, but often at the expense of the individual. Self-discipline is unpopular and unfashionable. It is difficult for the Church to pronounce on any issue without being harangued and told that it should get its own house in order, before telling others how to behave. Brian Fallon makes this pertinent point:

> At present Irish society, disillusioned and angry with a clergy which previously it had irrationally idealised and had deferred to blindly and uncritically, seems more likely to throw religion to the four winds than to take the more constructive, intelligent option of rethinking and regenerating it.[6]

Writing in *The Irish Times* on Friday, 13 August 1999, Kevin Myers warned against the danger of labelling men and women of the cloth as 'abusers' and 'sexual deviants'. He argues that the

Catholic Church was not an imposed hierarchy in Ireland but was, rather, indigenous. Thus, 'its norms, its disorders, its failings were well and truly authentically Irish'. He is correct. He goes on to make the point that I hinted at earlier: that homes throughout Ireland depended (and some still depend) on violence for the rule of order and the maintenance of hierarchy. Take away the Church and what are the Irish people left with? Very little apart from a spiritual and moral vacuum. We, unlike the French, depend on organised religion to give our lives some focus. As a people, we are still young, immature and insecure. The pub has replaced the home as the centre of familial contacts.

A different set of problems prevailed in France. The effects of the two world wars had been devastating, more particularly the second one, which had revealed France to be no longer a strong military or even moral force. The support given by the Catholic hierarchy to Maréchal Pétain, a devout Catholic with a romantic view of France's greatness, would be subjected to much scrutiny after the war. Had the French Catholic Church collaborated with the Nazi regime? Brian Moore's very interesting novel, *The Statement* (1996), tells of the tacit support given by many French priests and religious to a former milice[7] officer, Pierre Brossard, a thinly disguised portrayal of Paul Touvier who was tried for crimes against humanity in France in 1994. When reflecting on the state of post-war France, Brossard comes to the conclusion that he is shielded in monasteries and presbyteries all over the country because he did nothing wrong:

> How many in France knew then that we had not won but lost the battle? How many sensed it but didn't dare to say it? The Church knew: in Rome, Pius XII asked for an amnesty for all who had been faithful to the Maréchal

[Pétain]. The Pope knew the real enemy. He knew that the Maréchal was first and always a true son of the faith.[8]

Pius XII was very strong in his defence of traditional Catholicism and he had his admirers in France. He is also suspected of having had a pronounced anti-semitic bias and to have assisted the Nazis in their extermination of the Jews – he is referred to in some circles as the Hitler Pope. But there were other developments in France during the Second World War that would reveal a new approach to their vocation among certain clerics. In 1943 Cardinal Suhard received the manuscript of a book, *La France, pays de mission?*, which deeply moved him. One of the co-authors of the book, Henri Godin, was summoned to the cardinal's residence the following day. Suhard had already set up the 'Mission de France' in 1941, a seminary for young priests who were committed to carrying out their ministry among the working classes. In 1944 he set up the 'Mission de Paris' to look after the needs of the capital. In launching this initiative, Suhard was acknowledging the gap that had developed between the Church and the poor. Godin's book put forward the case that the French Church was a materialistic institution. To be a part of it, you needed to pay, and the more you paid, the better you were served. Suhard agreed with this theory and soon priests began to emerge from the Missions to become what were known as worker-priests. They were a source of outrage to many traditional Catholics, who saw them as out-of-control Marxists or crypto-Communists. But the worker-priests had a simple vocation, that of serving the poor. In so doing, they felt that they were merely continuing the work of Jesus Christ. After living for a while in high-rise flats and working at menial tasks, mostly in factories, the worker-priests began to see how Marxism, with its philosophy of the redistribution of wealth and equality for all, held a huge appeal for people who had long been kept in subservience. Pope Pius XII was disturbed to discover that many of these priests had become tinged with the Marxist cancer, that they rarely or never wore their clerical garb, that they used the vernacular when saying Mass. In 1953 he put an end to the worker-priests' experiment, feeling that it had gone too far. Many of the priests stayed on in their jobs and refused to return to a conventional ministry. There had only been ninety worker-priests in total and yet their influence was far greater than that of generations of priests before them. They had broken the mould, shown a fresh and authentic Christian witness. Their suppression was the expression of an inward-looking Roman curia, which needed to be visionary and outward-looking. This came with Vatican II some ten years later.

There were several highly-respected theologians and intellectuals in the French Church in the run-up to Vatican II. In fact, it is said that these men were responsible for the progressive and liberal course the Council followed on many issues. The contribution of the French lay philosopher, Jacques Maritain, whose views were welcomed in Vatican circles, should not be underestimated either. Daniélou, de Lubac, Congar – few countries outside of France could boast priests and theologians of their calibre. To those who claimed that the spiritual crisis that came after Vatican II was the fault of the Council, Yves Congar replied:

> For one thing, many of today's worrying realities could be sensed already in the 1950s, sometimes in the 1930s. The Council didn't bring them about in any way.... Vatican II was followed by a socio-economic mutation, whose intensity, radicality and speed had no equivalent in any other period of our history.[9]

Congar is correct in his assessment. The fall-off in religious practice during the sixties, seventies and eighties throughout the Western world can be explained by many factors over which the Council had no control. Think about it: the student revolts culminating in the famous protests in Paris in May 1968; the hippie generation with its motto 'Make love, not war'; the sexual revolution made possible to some degree (though to a very limited extent in Ireland) by the availability of artificial contraception; the reaction to the Korean and Vietnamese wars; the advent of the motorcar, which led to increased mobility; television and the images it brought to many households of a consumerist American society, which was viewed as the ideal that people should strive to emulate, all these developments would have come about with or without the Council. They had a huge impact on the Western world. Young people in particular were seeing other ways of looking at problems and were no longer prepared to accept unquestioningly the weekly sermons from priests who, during their training, had been deprived of newspapers, novels and electronic media. I have spoken to many former Maynooth seminarians of the seventy-year age group, who assure me that they never got to read a newspaper or a novel during their training. To then be faced with a congregation, many of whom were beginning to ask awkward questions and demand cogent answers, was for many young priests a nightmare. The monolithic authority of the Church was cracking. Authority was associated with power and the abuse of power and was thus ripe for challenge. John McGahern, in an interview, analysed Irish society in the following manner:

> The amazing thing is that it's a Catholic country and that nearly all the writers are not Catholics. They're lapsed Catholics. I think that the Church in Ireland was

peculiarly anti-intellectual, say, compared to the French Church. People like Mauriac or Bloy could have no place here. It was a simple world of the GAA and the drama society with a very distorted view of life.

Nobody actually took any time to understand what to be Irish was. There was this slogan and fanaticism and a lot of emotion, but there wasn't any clear idea except what you were against: you were against sexuality; you were against the English.[10]

True enough – but a lapsed Catholic is still a Catholic. The genes, the family loyalties, the symbols of sacrifice (in the Eucharist), the smells and the sounds survive in the inner consciousness and can resurface in strange ways. Yet the above quote is a fine analysis of the situation that pertained in Ireland for a long number of years. Many clergy were anti-intellectual and did nothing to encourage those in their care to assess what their faith consisted of. They spent a lot of time trying to ensure their control over the people by keeping control of schools and hospitals. They defined Catholic identity in negative terms: we were against sexuality and against the English. The Irish had been a downtrodden race for so long that we became subservient and unthinking. This suited a clergy whose greatest fear was revolt against their authority. Things have changed dramatically in the space of a few decades. Our entry into Europe in 1973 opened Ireland up to outside influences like never before. It also brought a new prosperity to the country, which is evidenced by the current economic boom, known as the Celtic Tiger. Materialism has brought in its wake secular values, atheism in many different forms. Mammon is the new God. This modern reality is not, however, reflected in the writings of the Irish novelists I have chosen to deal with in this book. They were all born into a repressive Irish society that was overwhelmingly Catholic, insular and conservative. Their experience of religion thus tended to be negative. To that extent they can seem outdated in the context of the twenty-first century. Nevertheless, they are a basic element in the Irish literature of the last century and they reflect in a meaningful way a society that moved from the claustrophobia experienced by Joyce and Beckett to the 'no-holds-barred' approach of today's writers. The French writers were writing in general for a public that had quite a strong anti-spiritual and anti-clerical bias and, in treating of religion, they were fighting against the tide of public mores to a certain extent. Much of what happened in France three or four decades ago can be seen in the Ireland of today. We can learn a lot from the French experience if we stop to think and reflect on it. In a survey carried out by the French magazine, *L'Express*, in 1994, it was pointed out that the vast majority of young people no longer possessed a sufficient religious vocabulary to recognise many biblical images and references in literature. Catholicism is the professed religion of eight out of ten French children, but its symbols are now almost completely foreign to them. (Can't you see the same thing happening in the next few decades in Ireland?) And yet the same survey notes heightened attraction among young people to the monastic life, to pilgrimages as well as to groups such as New Age and the oriental religions, Zen and Buddhism. There is an apparent paradox, as Michel de Certeau notes:

> On the one hand, the Church, as an organised structure, as a dogma and a hierarchial power, is weakening and sometimes appears to be dying on its feet. On the other hand, religion, or the spiritual, is everywhere.[11]

The human heart is restless without a God to meet its yearnings. The lesson learned in France is that the Church as an organised structure was never intended to be strong. It is only when it is weak that it is heard, loved and served by people who commit to it because they genuinely believe in what it has to offer. When reading through these essays I would ask you to apply many of the ideas that were current in France several years ago to the Ireland of today. I think you will find that they have more than a little relevance; a certain echo reverberates from them. This is why we chose the title of *Crosscurrents and Confluences*. When we speak of influence, it is apparent that it is the French novelists who influenced their Irish counterparts and not vice-versa. The French Catholic tradition, as embodied in writers of the distinction of Claudel, Péguy, Bloy, Bernanos, Mauriac, to mention just the best known, extended well beyond the boundaries of the Hexagon and is respected world-wide by believers and non-believers alike. This is because, apart from their Catholic beliefs, the French were first and foremost writers, and writers of genuine stature. We don't presume to place the Irish writers in the same category. However, they all, with the exception of McCourt, make references to the French literary tradition at some stage or another. Denis Sampson[12] makes some comparisons between McGahern and Proust. To my way of thinking, he is closer to Mauriac, due to the fascination his characters have with the land. (J. B. Keane deals with this preoccupation in a powerful and tragic way in *The Field*.) The manner in which Mauriac dealt dispassionately with the theme of religious hypocrisy among the land-owning classes living around Bordeaux struck a cord among readers here, especially during the fifties and sixties. The use of religion for social advancement and respectability was not far removed from our own experiences. But whereas the bulk of Mauriac's bourgeois characters are of well-to-do, landed families, in the novels of an author like McGahern they are generally small farmers and not very prosperous.

This does not seek to be an exhaustive study of religion in the French and Irish twentieth-century novel. Such a task would be a huge undertaking and one that might not yield rich results due to the differences, cultural and social, that mark the experiences of both countries. My plan is to deal with five French and five Irish novelists and to show how their works reveal some similarities and some discrepancies. Ireland and France have enjoyed close links down through the centuries and it is unavoidable that this has led to a cross-fertilisation of ideas on many issues. Brian Moore stated that he had a 'French cast of mind' and he readily admitted to being an admirer of Mauriac. He wondered why, in spite of his agnosticism, he kept writing about Catholics in his fiction. Belief or the absence of belief are ever-present in Moore's fiction. As Jo O'Donoghue points out:

> Though Mauriac is a novelist with whom he has been compared and with whom he has compared himself, Moore is the living denial of Mauriac's conviction about himself and other Catholics that 'He had not been free to choose or reject Catholicism for he was born a Catholic.'[13]

Moore abandoned the formal practice of religion at a young age and he no longer felt himself to be bound by the pronouncements of priests and bishops. His interest in those who had faith was constant throughout his life because he knew he never had that quality himself. For Moore, the fact that his icon, Joyce, had lived in France was very significant: 'I realised that writers were taken seriously in Europe, in a different way than they were in Ireland or England. I wanted to get away from the English thing. I wanted to be French!'[14] There is a sense in which all the Irish writers dealt with in this book would share Moore's sentiments about living in a country like France,

where the role of the writer has always been taken seriously.
Kate O'Brien studied French in UCD and stated that her
French professor, Roger Chauviré, revealed the study of
literature to be a serious adult occupation. She was deeply
attached to Flaubert, whom she regarded as the greatest novelist
of the nineteenth century. She also saw France as being 'the
European country where intellectuals and writers were taken for
granted, as much part of life as the green-grocer, the baker and
the haberdasher, French cooking not to be spoken of in the
same breath as other kinds of cooking'.[15] O'Brien also admitted
a predilection for Mauriac.

In the case of John Broderick, his friendship with Julien
Green and his broad knowledge of French literature brought
him on several occasions to Paris. At a John Broderick
commemorative weekend organised by the Athlone Rotary
Club to mark the tenth year since the death of the author in
1989, Brian Fallon noted: 'He [Broderick] not only knew and
loved French literature, he loved the French language itself and
was one of the relatively few of his generation who spoke it well
– the poet John Montague is another. He had lived for periods
in France, he understood its social nuances and its family life,
he loved French wine and food and he also knew a number of
French writers personally.' Broderick was steeped in the novels
of Mauriac and admired the poetry of Charles Baudelaire, a
type of Catholic blasphemer. Fallon explains why Broderick,
and I think the same holds true for some of the other Irish
writers I deal with, was more at home in France than in Ireland:
'People like him, who were closer to the French tradition which
gives far more liberty to the individual and does not regard
questioning of accepted dogma as deserving of Hell fire, were
often at odds with the more fundamentalist form [of
Catholicism] they had grown up with.' Broderick also read and
understood Proust, a not insignificant achievement!

Frank McCourt is the one writer who doesn't show any obvious signs of having undergone the French influence. He has spent most of his life in the United States and looked to Joyce more than to any French model for his inspiration. Nevertheless, in his treatment of religion in the Limerick of his youth, he is an indispensable reference point for this book. People will justifiably bemoan my failure to include novelists whom they find relevant to the theme. My answer to them is: where does one draw the line? My decision to choose just ten writers was determined by my reading preferences and limited expertise in the area. I seek to draw the reader's attention to some novelists who are already very well known and about whom several books have been written, and others whom I feel have never got the recognition they deserved. This book falls between two stools, literary criticism and socio-religious discussion. I hope therefore that it will have something for both the experts and the uninitiated.

As long as humankind exists on earth, the search for the meaning of such an existence will continue. The mind boggles at the concept of eternity yet it cannot ignore its existence unless it accepts non-existence as the successor of death. If one does that, it places the human being on the same level as plants and animals – thinking men and women tend generally to find such a scenario unacceptable. The theologian, the philosopher, the psychologist, the poet, continue to search and search, but perhaps the novelist is the one who leads the way as he/she has the freedom, the initiative and the vision to see the lives of men and women as the never-ceasing quest for a meaning for life. Let us now consider how our French and Irish novelists tackle this challenge.

NOTES

1. I should add that in the early years of the national seminary in Maynooth a good number of the professors were French. The impact of this on the young men training for the priesthood would have been considerable, especially as most of them had only basic education before becoming aspirants to the priesthood. In the nineteenth and early twentieth centuries the priest and the primary teacher were the leaders in rural communities, and such communities included the vast majority of the Irish population until Seán Lemass's drive for industrialisation led to the growth of cities and towns and the decimation of many rural communities. Emigration to the United States, Australia, and later to Great Britain, did the rest.

2. Letter to Thomas Mac Greevy, 31 January 1938. Quoted by Declan Kiberd, *Inventing Ireland* (London: Jonathan Cape, 1995), p. 580.

3. Dermot Keogh, *Twentieth Century Ireland: Nation and State* (Dublin: New Gill History of Ireland 6, 1996), p. 70.

4. Jean Sulivan, *Anticipate Every Farewell.* This is my translation of the French text, *Devance tout adieu,* which describes the relationship of Jean Sulivan, a priest, with his dying mother. It also provides a very keen insight into religious practice in Brittany at the turn of the century. Veritas hopes to publish this translation in the near future.

5. Tony Flannery, *From the Inside. A Priest's View of the Catholic Church* (Cork: Mercier, 1999), p. 14.

6. Brian Fallon, *An Age of Innocence: Irish Culture 1930-1960* (Dublin: Gill & Macmillan, 1998), p. 28. This is an indispensable reference for anyone wishing to understand the intricacies of this period. Fallon is particularly fair in his assessment of how Irish people are being rather hasty in their rush to destroy any possible role for the Catholic Church in Ireland. It would obviously be better to contribute to changing and regenerating it than abandoning it completely. Fallon does accept, however, that the Church in many ways contributed to its own alienation: 'In its intolerance of any opposition, its inability to accept criticism from others or to criticise itself, lay the seeds of the Church's dilemma today. Thanks to an overwhelming Catholic majority, it had no organised anti-clerical groupings to contend with, no equivalent of the old Radical Party in France, nothing which would have kept it alert, self-aware and sensitive to changing circumstances and modernist currents' (p. 197).

7. Military police set up by the Nazis in France and composed in the main of French officers. They were responsible for some notorious atrocities against Jews during World War II.

8. Brian Moore, *The Statement* (London: Flamingo, 1996), p. 22.

9. Yves Congar, *La Parole et le souffle* (Paris: Desclée de Brouwer, 1984), p. 69.

10. In Julia Carson (ed.), *Banned in Ireland. Censorship and the Irish Writer* (Athens: University of Georgia Press, 1990), p. 63.

11. Michel de Certeau, *Le Christianisme éclaté* (Paris: Seuil, 1974), pp. 13-14.

12. Denis Sampson, *Outstaring Nature's Eye. The Fiction of John McGahern* (Washington: Catholic University of America Press, 1993).

13. Jo O'Donoghue, *Brian Moore: A Critical Study* (McGill-Queen's University Press, 1991), p. 9.

14. 'The Life of Brian.' Interview with Joe O'Connor, *The Sunday Tribune*, 1 October, 1995.

15. Lorna Reynolds, *Kate O'Brien: A Literary Portrait* (Colin Smythe Limited, 1987), p. 35.

1

THE SEARCH FOR AUTHENTICITY IN FRANÇOIS MAURIAC'S *THÉRÈSE DESQUEYROUX*

François Mauriac (1885-1970) is the type of writer one approaches almost with reverence because of his canonical position in French and European literary circles. Born of well-to-do bourgeois stock in Bordeaux in 1885, his literary reputation was established from the moment he submitted his first collection of poetry, *Les Mains Jointes*, to Maurice Barrès in 1909, who predicted: 'You will have a glorious career!' Such literary intuition was subsequently proved to be correct. Elected to the Académie Française in 1937, Mauriac won the Nobel Prize for literature in 1952. Known as a writer with a keen insight into how the unconscious functions, he is also recognised as a distinctly Catholic writer. Like all the French writers we meet in this book who have had this tag applied to their work, Mauriac refused to allow his literary output to be summarised in such a simplistic manner. For someone considered such a strongly Catholic writer, he did, in fact, struggle to convince some of his Catholic readers that what he wrote was compatible with his religious convictions. In *Le Roman* (The Novel), which attempts to explain his approach to fiction, Mauriac stated that at the beginning of the twentieth century it was necessary for French writers to move out of the shadow of Balzac, whose characters are confined to the role of types, and move closer to the dark light of Dostoevsky, whose novels are remarkable for their illogicality. What attracts Mauriac to the Russian writer's characters is how the sublime and the vile seem to complement their actions. He says:

> It is not because Dostoevsky's heroes are Russian that they appear so disturbing to many French readers. It is rather because they are men so like us, that is to say chaotic beings, individuals that are so filled with contradictions that we don't know what to think of them. This is because Dostoevsky doesn't impose any order or logic on them other than the logic of life, which from the point of view of our reason is the essence of illogicality.[1]

Whereas Balzac's characters fulfil the role assigned to them, those of Dostoevsky escape from the expectations of both the writer and the readers. Mauriac felt that this was the truest form of portrayal; that it was not possible in many cases to predict what way human nature will work in certain situations. He expressed a liking for those among his characters who wouldn't submit to his will, who resisted the roles he tried to impose on them. At times he wondered if the very act of writing was compatible with the state of grace. He expressed the dangers to which he believed his writings exposed him:

> A Catholic writer advances along a narrow crest between two chasms: he cannot be a cause of scandal and yet he cannot lie either; he must not excite the desires of the flesh, and yet he must also beware of not giving a false picture of life. Which is the greater danger: making young people dream in an aberrant manner or inspiring disgust in them for Christ and His Church?[2]

What is always apparent in Mauriac is his commitment to depict human nature in as honest and realistic a manner as possible, regardless of the consequences. His novels are written in a style that is clear, concise and economical. Brian Fallon, in his Introduction to this book, speaks of the fall-off in Mauriac's once-commanding position among the reading public: this is true to an extent. Yet there are very few French people who haven't read at least one of his novels and his literary gifts are almost universally acknowledged. The world he portrays, however, with its land-owning classes and devious, evil characters, no longer speaks as obviously to French people or to Europeans in general. The traditional French rural life as portrayed in Mauriac's writings has all but disappeared. All over the country, small rural towns and villages are becoming deserted by all but a handful of elderly inhabitants. In Ireland, where a similar migration has begun, we can still relate to Mauriac's settings. We can also identify with many of his characters who, although they profess to be genuine and committed Catholics, see no contradiction between their religious convictions and swindling people out of money or land. Theirs is a pragmatic and unspiritual type of religion, not that far removed from the hard-headed type of religious practice that prevailed in Ireland until recently and that can still be sensed on occasions even among the liberal consumerists. Religion dies hard even when it is being subverted.

Mauriac is a significant figure in this book for several reasons. Firstly, three of the Irish novelists explored in these pages cited Mauriac as an influence on their writings. In addition, there is the fact that he is a major reference point in terms of world Catholic literature. I use the term 'Catholic literature' with reluctance because I am aware of the danger of misinterpretation. J. C. Whitehouse[3] quotes the critic, Gonzague Truc,[4] who argues that the most strongly Catholic literature is not a confessional literature, where the author is simply a preacher or an apologist. Catholicism, unconsciously or consciously, informs the writings of those who have been brought up with a knowledge of its doctrines and dogmas.

Whitehouse adds:

> In other words [he's interpreting Truc's thesis], Catholic novels, like all other works of literary art which incorporate a specific doctrine or system, share in the major advantage which art has over polemics, which is that they present experience rather than arguments drawn from experience. Whatever the message involved, it is the conviction and power of the experience portrayed which will determine what the reader's deepest reaction will be.[5]

The process resembles an unconscious parable. When reading Mauriac's novels, I never get the impression that I am being preached at. In many instances it is not even apparent to me that the author is a Catholic. This is because what matters first and foremost to Mauriac is 'the conviction and power of the experience portrayed'. It should be remembered that Mauriac's writings reveal a spiritual anguish and a constant questioning of his faith. His deeply held spiritual convictions did not prevent him in his novels and journalistic articles from launching scathing attacks on the pharisaic attitude of many Catholics, attacks that would have done credit to his republican/secular enemies. In many cases these diatribes were also directed at himself, as he knew that he had not escaped from the sins of his class and caste. He aroused anger among some Catholics for his depiction of the hypocrisy of the bourgeois class, for whom religion had more to do with social standing than with any sincere search for the truth. He may have loved the hypocrites as individuals but he hated the hypocrisy – 'Hate the sin but love the sinner'.

Authenticity was all-important to Mauriac, and many of his characters, especially the ones to whom he was most attached, share with their creator an inability to hide behind a mask, to conform to social mores. Thérèse Desqueyroux is a striking example of a Mauriacian character, who rebels against the role assigned to her after she gets married. Thérèse turns to crime as a means of possible revenge for the fate that befalls her. When Mauriac displays sympathy for this woman who attempts to poison her husband, he knows that he is treading on dangerous ground. In the Foreword of the novel, he seeks to explain his position:

> Many will feel surprise that I should give imagined life to a creature more odious than any character in my other books. Why, they will ask, have I never anything to say to those who ooze with virtue and who 'wear their hearts on their sleeves'? People who 'wear their hearts on their sleeves' have no story for me to tell, but I know the secrets of the hearts that are deep buried in, and mingled with, the filth of flesh.[6]

Mauriac understood the meaning of human frailty. He is already preparing the reader for the story of a woman whose destiny 'is mingled with the filth of flesh', someone who is far from virtuous, who is, in fact, a potential murderess and for whom Mauriac has obvious sympathy. The novel opens after Thérèse's trial for the attempted murder of her husband. We are introduced to a feeble, pale woman with a high forehead who seems 'condemned to an eternity of loneliness' (p. 18). And this in spite of the fact that the case against her has been dismissed. Her lawyer accompanies her to a meeting with her father, a local politician, who hides himself in the shadows for fear of being spotted in public in the company of his criminal daughter. His concern is that the trial may have damaged his political reputation and he talks to the lawyer as though Thérèse were not there. When she tentatively suggests that she might spend a few days with him in his house, he baulks at the idea, saying that it is more vital than ever now that she and her husband be seen as a united couple.

Thérèse thus prepares the 'confession' she will make to Bernard. During the train journey to Argelouse,[7] the country residence where her husband is convalescing, she contemplates the events that led up to her crime. She realises that her marriage to Bernard had been her long-cherished ambition. The estates of the two families were adjoining and seemed made for fusion. She had property in her blood and was attracted to Bernard because of his wealth and standing – so her motives for getting married were far from pure. But a marriage based on property did not yield happiness. Bernard was your typical country squire, interested mainly in hunting, eating and ensuring that the estate was making a tidy profit. He didn't possess his wife's intellectual prowess and, in fact, thought very little about any abstract issues. From a very early stage it was obvious to Thérèse that the union did not bring her fulfilment:

> Everything which dates from before my marriage I see now as bathed in a light of purity – doubtless because that time stands out in such vivid contrast to the indelible filth of my wedded life. (p. 22)

Purity is despoiled, even within the sacramental bounds of matrimony. Mauriac was tainted with a Jansenistic view of sexuality, which sees sexual love as an obstacle to the love of God. Many Irish writers, we will see, shared this pessimistic view of the fallen character of human nature. Purity can only exist, apparently, before any sexual act has been engaged in. Thérèse realises that the problem lies not so much with her husband as with herself. She sees her life extending in front of her like:

> An endless tunnel, that I was driving ahead into a darkness that grew more dense the further I advanced, so that I sometimes wondered whether I should suffocate before I reached the open air again. (pp. 64-5)

If this were not bad enough, things are further exacerbated by the news, received at the end of their honeymoon, that her great friend and sister-in-law, Anne de la Trave, has fallen in love with Jean Azévédo. Thérèse, on reading Anne's passionate account of this romance in a series of letters, cannot help comparing it to the sterility of her own relationship with Bernard. The following is the graphic description she gives of the sexual act:

> Nothing is so severing as the frenzy that seizes upon our partner in the act. I always saw Bernard as a man who charged head-down at pleasure, while I lay like a corpse, motionless, as though fearing that, at the slightest gesture on my part, this madman, this epileptic, might strangle me. (p. 35)

If there was any doubt about Mauriac's Jansenism in the previous quotation, it is all too apparent in descriptions such as the one above. Thérèse, in this similar to many of Mauriac's characters, is incapable of dissociating the flesh from sin. The sexual act is reduced to a type of animalistic ritual to which she is forced to submit. She sees Bernard as a beast in the throes of passion: 'a madman, an epileptic.' Marriage has legitimised this sort of behaviour. One might well wonder how Mauriac developed this type of suspicious attitude to the flesh. Some insights can be gleaned from his autobiographical account of his childhood, *Commencements d'une vie*. In it, we are told of how his father died when Mauriac was twenty months old (the premature loss of a parent is a common thread running though most of our authors) and thus the child's relationship with his mother became very intense. Madame Mauriac was a very devout Catholic and sought to imbue a respect for their bodies in her children:

> Our nightgowns were so long that I couldn't even get to scratch my foot. We knew that the Lord above demanded from His children that they sleep with their arms crossed over their chests. We went to sleep with our arms folded, our palms almost nailed against our bodies, grasping the holy medals and the scapular of Mount Carmel that we couldn't remove, even in the bath. The five children thus hugged against their bodies, in an embrace that was already passionate, the invisible love of God.[8]

Such rituals serve to reinforce a negative attitude to their bodies in young people and it certainly appears to have left its mark on Mauriac. Likewise Thérèse, though a liberal thinker in many respects, cannot escape shuddering when it comes to contemplating sex. She is asked by the family to intervene on its behalf with Anne, to convince her that an affair and possible marriage to a consumptive degenerate of Jewish origin will serve no useful purpose. Respectability and appearances were the guiding factors in the life of Bernard and in that of his family.[9] The family unit was sacrosanct and individual will had to give way to collective reasoning. Thérèse, on Anne's request, meets with Azévédo. To her surprise, she discovers that he has no real interest in Anne. He talks instead about Paris, his literary friends, the life he leads. He listens to Thérèse's opinions, which Bernard never does, and treats her as an equal. A few months into her first pregnancy, Thérèse is gratified, even slightly embarrassed, by the attentions of this young man whose life is so different from hers.

The way the family regard her with respect now that she 'bore within her the future master of unnumbered trees' (p. 44), the hypocrisy she sees in all their posturing about Anne's relationship, her pregnancy, her meeting with Jean Azévédo, all these elements contributed to her decision to poison her husband. She felt as though she were suffocating in the mundane provincial life that she was compelled to lead. Her suffocation included revulsion to the sexual act. Like Madame Bovary, she had a romantic addiction to the Grand Passion but, unlike Flaubert's character, hers was an emotional and cerebral, non-physical experience. Also, Thérèse possesses an intelligence and perceptiveness with which poor Emma was never endowed.

Mauriac shows all his sharpness as a psychologist in his description of Thérèse's criminal act. The bulk of the novel deals with the 'preparation' of the confession she will make to her husband. It is here that the catharsis begins. She appears to be even more of a victim than Bernard, incapable as she is of controlling the evil within her. Bernard, being something of a hypochondriac, had begun taking arsenic drops for a slight heart complaint. On a very warm and sultry summer's day, when everyone was preoccupied by the fire in the nearby forest in Mano, he entered the room and took two drops of arsenic. Thérèse noticed him doing so and realised that he had already taken his daily dose: 'She said nothing, partly because she was too lazy to speak, partly too, no doubt, because she was tired' (p. 74). The narrator is careful to let the reader know that there was nothing premeditated in her inaction. She was sleepy and distracted, too tired to speak. That night, Bernard was terribly sick. When the doctor came, Thérèse neglected to tell him about the extra drops. She was now embarked on a course of action over which she would have no control. Like one of Dostoevsky's characters, there is no inherent logic to her behaviour. She systematically sets out to poison her husband.

The reader observes her action with a good deal of sympathy. Bernard is obsessed with himself and with his position in the local community; he is lacking in sensitivity towards his wife, is opinionated and arrogant. He represents in Thérèse's eyes not just the suffocation of marriage but also the suffocation of hypocrisy. It is not hard to imagine how difficult it would be for his wife, with her clear-sightedness and dislike of humbug, to endure him. His hypocrisy is best illustrated on the day of the Corpus Christi procession, which Thérèse watches, fascinated by the mystical traits of the young priest, who seems to be in contact with another world. She contrasts this spiritual fervour with Bernard, who is almost the only man walking behind the canopy and who imagines himself to be 'doing his duty' (p. 73). The words are in inverted commas in the text in order to underline Bernard's lack of sincerity.

Thérèse too has her faults – of that there can be no doubt. But at least she has the merit of being able to make critical observations about herself; Bernard worries only about how he is perceived by others. He uses religion as a means of strengthening his feeling of respectability and moral superiority. The heroine realises that it is unrealistic to expect forgiveness from a man as convinced of his virtue as her husband is.[10] Sure enough, when she reaches Argelouse, instead of being given the opportunity to explain her actions, she is forced to listen to her husband laying down the law. They will be seen together on certain important family occasions, as social convention demands, he says. He did not testify against her for the simple reason that it might damage their daughter's future. Although their marriage is over, they will continue to keep up appearances.

That night, after her husband has finally stopped talking, Thérèse is left alone in her room, where she actively considers ending her life. She wonders what death will be like and cannot convince herself that there is nothing and nobody after mortality. She decides to lay down a challenge to God:

> If that being did exist... since he *did* exist, let him prevent the criminal act while there was still time. Or, if it was his will that a poor blind soul should open for itself a way to death, let him at least receive with love the monster he had made. (p. 90)

Before she can take the poison that will end her life, she is interrupted by the sudden commotion in the house and the news that her Aunt Clara has been found dead in her bed. A prayer answered? It would appear so. Some critics maintain that the death of Clara, who had a genuine affection for her niece, is a sacrifice made to save Thérèse, a substitution of souls if you like. Certainly, Mauriac would argue that his heroine is deserving of God's mercy. He admires her lack of dissemblance, her search for authenticity. The fact that she had never really been loved by anyone (apart from her aunt) had made her into a monster. There is much evidence in the Bible to suggest that Jesus did not merely reserve grace for the just, that sinners also benefited from divine mercy.[11] Through her suffering and great inner turmoil, Thérèse achieves something approaching happiness at the end of the novel. After an absence of a couple of months, Bernard rejoins his wife in Argelouse. Anne, cured of her infatuation with Azévédo, is now prepared to marry the man the family has chosen for her, a local landowner called Deguilhem. (Anne's rebellion is short-lived, because she is essentially her parents' child). Deguilhem wishes to meet Thérèse, about whom many rumours have been circulating, before his engagement to Anne becomes official. Bernard is astonished at the physical deterioration he perceives in his wife. She has been very ill, in part due to the neglect of the servants but mainly because of her lack of will to live, the realisation of the evil within her and her inability to fight it. She is a broken woman.

The metaphor of the cage is very strong in Mauriac's descriptions of the sequestration of Thérèse in Argelouse. She is trapped, suffocating without hope. She is even deprived of her one consolation, her cigarettes, because the servants fear that in her carelessness she will set fire to the bed. In spite of her weakness, Thérèse manages to play the role of dutiful wife in front of Deguilhem. When the latter has left, Bernard rebukes the servants for neglecting his wife in such a manner. As a reward for her 'fine performance', Thérèse is allowed to move to Paris, after Anne's wedding. One would expect this to be a source of great joy to a woman for whom a cosmopolitan city held the promise of a life of freedom and the pursuit of culture. But this is not the case. Had Bernard asked her to come back with him to Bordeaux (he had accompanied her to Paris in another attempt to preserve appearances), she would have consented to do so:

> She played in imagination with the idea of going back to the sad and secret land – of spending a lifetime of meditation and self-discipline in the silence of Argelouse, there to set forth on the great adventure of the human soul, the search for God. (p. 109)

God is mentioned by name only very rarely in this book. However, Thérèse, without being outwardly religious, does invoke him in her hour of need, as evidenced by her prayer prior to taking the lethal dose of poison. Her opinion of religion is warped by her proximity to people who have not even begun to question their beliefs, who live a lie. Mauriac's heroine is turned into a psychological ogre by the failure of people with whom she comes in contact to understand or to love her. There is also a strong rebellious streak in her, a desire to shock people out of their complacency, a refusal to conform. 'To thine own self be true': these words are a fitting epitaph to this woman's life. She seeks an authentic path and is constantly faced with obstacles and pitfalls. She does not know what answer to give Bernard when he asks her why she tried to poison him. He attributes the attempt to a desire to acquire all their property for herself. This shows how little he knows about his wife.

> What I wanted? she says. It would be a great deal easier to tell you what I didn't want. I didn't want to be forever playing a part, to go through a series of movements, to continue speaking words that were not my own: in short, to deny at every moment of the day a Thérèse who.... (pp. 112-13)

She sees that Bernard is not going to accept this explanation. For him, everything has to be simplified and he cannot even begin to comprehend the complexity of another human being. What is worse is that he does not even want to. So he leaves her on the pavement in Paris. She thinks with some excitement about what lies ahead of her. She is now ready to commence a new period in her life, a new stage in her search for authenticity in the midst of all the chaos and confusion.

Thérèse Desqueyroux marks a high point in Mauriac's literary accomplishments. In its intensity and drama, it resembles a Greek tragedy. Thérèse is the tragic heroine who brings a dreadful fate down upon herself. At times we have the impression that she has no control over her actions, that she is in a type of trance. And yet, through the subtle probings of the novelist, we begin to see an unhappy and unfortunate woman who attempts to break out of an artificial existence. When she says to Bernard, by way of explaining her foiled attempt to poison him: 'I was the victim of a terrible duty. Yes, honestly, I had the feeling that it was a duty' (p. 111), we see that she has a point, that people's motivations are obscure and tantalising, that the most terrible deeds can sometimes appear justifiable.

Mauriac anticipated a bad reaction to his evoking of sympathy for a woman who attempted murder. And yet literature contains many examples of this type of depiction. One has but to think of the serial killer Macbeth, for whom Shakespeare evoked sympathy, or Dostoevsky's Raskolnikov. The evil person is much more attractive artistically than the good person. Unlike Bernanos, who dared to depict saintly priests and at the same time maintained the reader's willing suspension of disbelief, Mauriac was more at home when dealing with people who were engulfed in evil. He realised that this might seem inconsistent with his strong Catholic convictions but, as he said in *Le Romancier et ses personnages* about Thérèse and his other best-known character, Louis (*Le Noeud de Vipères*):

> …as distasteful as they appear to many, they are free of the one thing I detest above all else in the world and which I have difficulty enduring in any human being: complacency, a feeling of self-righteousness. They are not happy with themselves, they know their own misery.[12]

'Knowing your own misery', accepting your faults, are essential qualities in the quest for authenticity. And this quest for authenticity, is it not in many ways a seeking out of God? Thérèse plumbs the depths of anguish before she can bear to look on herself without loathing. Her itinerary is in some ways a spiritual awakening but the novelist leaves her when she is on the point of conversion. What is important above all else is the search, the beginnings of self-consciousness and the presence of a Creator. What happens afterwards between God and his creature is not the domain of the novelist, in Mauriac's estimation. Under the pseudonym Donat O'Donnell, Conor Cruise O'Brien, writing about Mauriac in 1953, noted how he may have lacked the intellectual gifts of Sartre or Camus in developing a theme, but that he far outstripped them when it came to depicting his inner torment and the delight he took in it. He concluded with a prophesy that still holds good almost half a century later:

> The power of transmuting such torment and delight into a communicable form is very rare, and those who possess it will find readers and admirers as long as humanity continues to enjoy tormenting itself. That will perhaps be longer than the theoreticians of 'anguish' can hold their large but restless audience.[13]

Yet the novelist has a charter to plumb depths in the human psyche that are not within the remit of the philosopher or the theologian. Psychology is a relatively new science which has learned much about the inner, often unconscious workings of that mystery we call the human mind from the great novelists. Mauriac is a splendid exemplar of just that potential and of the continuing achievement of the creative writer who is bold, challenging, sympathetic and searching.

NOTES

1. F. Mauriac, *Le Roman* (Paris: L'Artisan du Livre, 1928), pp. 51-52.

2. Ibid., p. 80.

3. J. C. Whitehouse, 'Catholic Writing: Some Basic Notions, Some Criticisms, and a Tentative Reply', in *Modern Language Review*, 73, 2, 1978.

4. G. Truc, *Histoire de la littérature catholique contemporaine* (Tournai: 1961), p. 290.

5. J. C. Whitehouse, op. cit.

6. F. Mauriac, *Thérèse Desqueyroux*, Penguin Modern Classics (London: Methuen, 1972), p. 9. All my references will be from this edition.

7. Argelouse is the property of Thérèse's Aunt Clara, the spinster with whom the heroine liked to spend her summer holidays during adolescence. Aunt Clara was a mother-figure to Thérèse, whose biological mother had died when she was very young. After their marriage, she and Bernard continued to spend quite a deal of time there.

8. *Commencements d'une vie*, in *Oeuvres complètes*, Tome I, Edition (de la Pléiade, NRF, Gallimard, 1990), p. 70.

9. We see from his behaviour after the trial that her own father shares this view.

10. Malcolm Scott (*The Struggle for the Soul of the French Novel. French Catholic and Realist Novelists 1850-1970* [London: Macmillan Press, 1989], p. 196) notes that the train journey to Argelouse is a mirror of the interior journey she makes into the depths of her character and that 'it does nothing to lighten her burden of despair, for her proposed confession (to Bernard) is a secular one, unable to provide the relief of its sacramental counterpart.' After all, 'Bernard is not a priest; the absolution she craves cannot come from him, but only from God, through the mediation of the Church'.

11. ' I have come, not to call the upright but sinners to repentance' (Luke 5:10, 32).

12. *Le Romancier et ses personnages*, in Edmond Jaloux, *François Mauriac romancier* (Editions Buchet/Chastel, 1984), pp. 117-18.

13. Donat O'Donnell, *Maria Cross. Imaginative Patterns in a Group of Modern Catholic Writers* (London: Chatto & Windus, 1953), p. 37.

2

GRACE IN BERNANOS' *DIARY OF A COUNTRY PRIEST*

It is impossible to speak of religion and the twentieth-century French novel without mentioning Georges Bernanos (1888-1948). Here is a writer who died relatively young – in his sixtieth year – and whose literary output consists of novels, polemical essays and a rich correspondence – he was a great letter writer. Bernanos was offered a chair in the Académie Française, which he refused, in spite of the fact that such an elevation would have eased his financial difficulties, which were considerable.

He was always afraid of compromising his principles by becoming a member of the literary establishment, which may explain some of the tension between himself and Mauriac. The latter was one of the main movers in trying to get Bernanos to change his mind about the Académie.

The standard of his writings is uneven. In some novels, like *Sous le soleil de Satan* (1926), he gave full vent to his prejudices and dislikes. He caricatured the writer Anatole France, as well as having a swipe at the bourgeois family of the heroine, Mouchette Malorthy, who are taken in by the denials of the dissolute Marquis de Cardignan that he is having an affair with their daughter. Bernanos feels no sympathy for the plight of the Malorthys, who are Republicans, and who unwittingly subject their daughter to even further danger by sending her to consult the local doctor, Gallet, a public representative; he also has evil designs on her person. The father explains why he trusts Gallet:

After all, a doctor represents learning, science... he's not merely a man. He's the high priest of a true Republican.[1]

The irony here is transparent. Bernanos intrudes excessively in this manner in many of his novels, in order to belittle his adversaries. He felt obliged to rail against naturalism, especially as he envisaged this phenomenon in the writings of Zola – he never forgave the latter for his defence of Dreyfus. He also had disdain for Republicans because of their abandoning of Catholicism for the religion of science and politics. However, he was much more experimental in his writings from the aesthetic point of view than Mauriac and used disturbing dream sequences and an unclear narrative in some of his novels. For example, *Monsieur Ouine* is a type of detective novel which portrays the mayhem that takes place in a small provincial town that is totally apathetic to the affairs of the spirit and where murder, rape, homosexuality and lunacy are hinted at rather than described. There is a lack of any conventional story-line and much is conveyed by dream sequences and disjointed narrative. We are talking here about a *nouveau roman d'avant la lettre* (a new novel before such a concept came into being). The novelistic techniques employed by Bernanos have been subjected to much scrutiny by literary experts and they are indeed interesting. However, his current popularity in France owes more to his spirituality than to any aesthetic reasons. This of itself is a bit confusing, given the move away from institutional religion in that country. Conservative in religious matters to the point of fanaticism, Bernanos' characters, especially the priests, have an other-worldliness, whose appeal never seems to wane. The film version of *Sous le soleil de Satan (Under Satan's Sun)* elicited a fine performance from Gérard Depardieu in the main role and was a commercial success in the 1980s. When I attempt to explain the special appeal of

Bernanos' writings I always come back to his depiction of grace, the theme of this particular chapter. It is best seen and understood in one of his later works, *The Diary of a Country Priest*. This novel shows an artistic reserve that is lacking in his more polemical writings and what we get in it is a genuine insight into the spiritual itinerary of an ordinary priest who has an extraordinary interiority. Before embarking on a discussion of this theme I think that Malcolm Scott captures the importance of Bernanos' contribution to the Catholic novel in France when he writes:

> Whatever one thinks of Bernanos' beliefs, his attempts to house them in novels challenges all the assumptions about the nature of novels that the twentieth century inherited from the nineteenth. The struggle for the soul of the novel here reaches its point of greatest intensity.[2]

No other French writer has captured as well as Bernanos the *mystery* of grace. When you try to come to grips with it, it eludes you like mercury or fairy gossamer. It may only strike one at odd moments – like when you witness a red sunset inundating a furze-covered mountain, or a friend opening her eyes after an accident, or the sound of Mozart on a sultry morning, or the first cry of a newborn baby. These moments are natural embodiments of grace and come uncalled for by any religious motivation. But so too does grace. The problems arise for a novelist when s/he attempts to portray how the supernatural operates on the human soul. More often than not, if one is not exceptionally talented, the attempt will fall on its feet because it will appear didactic or sanctimonious. We have writers like Graham Greene and Flannery O'Connor, who tried to come to terms with grace in their writings, but in an oblique manner. No one has tackled the subject more forcibly than

Bernanos, the writer whose name is synonymous with the Catholic novel in France. One might expect that, having fallen into disuse, this type of novel is no longer attracting a wide readership. Maybe it's out of date, irrelevant to the modern mindset. This can certainly not be said of Bernanos, whose writings, especially his *Diary of a Country Priest*, have a prophetic quality that is fresh and universal. Like all good literature, it has stood the test of time.

His literary world is fused through and through with Catholicism. Two of his best-loved and most admired heroes, Donissan *(Under Satan's Sun)* and the curé d'Ambricourt *(The Diary of a Country Priest)*, are priests. The supernatural and the mystical are major elements in his characters' lives. Sin and grace, salvation and perdition, God and Satan, good and evil, recur as central themes. Whereas in Mauriac the psychological recesses of the soul are examined minutely, almost microscopically, the novelist evaded an analysis of the workings of grace. Mauriac knew that his attempts at evoking grace met with failure and that he was more comfortable with capturing souls enveloped in sin. When reading Bernanos, it is necessary to have some insights into Catholic theology to appreciate the motivation of his characters. The dramatic situations they face are far-reaching in their consequences: wrong decisions could bring about eternal damnation. Satan is working constantly in a demonic world where religion is declining as a social and spiritual force. At times the Prince of Evil appears to be winning in the struggle against God. It is all very dramatic, as powerful in its own way as Milton's portrayal of Satan and of Hell.

Georges Bernanos was a Catholic and his novels possess a clearly 'Catholic' tone, but he was in no sense a front man for the Church. In fact, he was not slow to point out faults which he saw in the institution or to criticise its abuses at times. His prophetic vision gave him a glimpse into what the French

Church would look like: with a decrease in religious fervour, the growing influence of secular and materialistic values, fewer priests, widespread spiritual inertia. His prophecy is well on its way to fulfilment. By 1943, Henri Godin, in the pamphlet of which he was co-author, *France un pays de mission?*, was able to state that France had become a missionary country, that the Church had lost the working classes to Marxism. Vatican II sought to open the Church to the modern world. Its documents alienated many sincere traditional Catholics in France, who didn't see the necessity for change. (We don't need to be reminded of the support, tacit or otherwise, that Archbishop Lefèbvre received in his own country.) The conference of French bishops at Lourdes in 1978 announced that only ninety-nine priests were ordained in the previous year.[3] The situation has not improved since. The attentive reader of Bernanos should not be surprised at such an outcome. A close look at his most famous novel, *The Diary of a Country Priest*, reveals that as early as the 1930s the French Church was heading for irrelevance as well as hostility.

The Diary was published by Plon in 1936. It is set in a rural parish, Ambricourt, where evil seems to be in control. It is to this parish that the young priest is sent. He is immediately upset by the 'ennui' which he senses in his surroundings:

> I wonder if man has ever before experienced this contagion, this leprosy of boredom: an aborted despair, a shameful form of despair in some way like the fermentation of Christianity in decay.[4]

The French 'ennui' means more than simple 'boredom'. It evokes an aura of spiritual lethargy, an existentialist anguish that possesses the mind and the soul. Ambricourt parish is in some ways a microcosm of French society in the 1930s, a society in which Christianity was 'in decay'. The naïve curé struggles to win back some of the influence lost by the Church. But his efforts at evangelising are met with hostility and disdain. He is tricked by tradesmen, says Mass in an empty church, and fails to secure the good will or support of the local landlord. He is an inefficient administrator; too soft, too self-effacing, too servile. And yet he is living a strong inner life of self-sacrifice and has the sensitivity to detect pain and suffering among his parishioners.

The doctor, Delbende, who 'would hurl questions at a crucifix hanging on his bedroom wall' (p. 90), has a problem with the Church's attitude to the poor. One day he challenges the curé:

> The fact remains that a poor man, a real poor man, an honest man, goes of his own accord to what he considers his proper place, the lowest in the house of the Lord. (p. 63)

He needn't have bothered: the curé knew poverty and the abuse of the poor from his early childhood.[5] He does not rebel against penury; rather he sees it as a way of identifying more closely with the passion of Christ, who chose to endure the darkness of pain, humiliation and death so that his people might live in his light. The curé has no glib answers for Delbende. Instead, he opts to take his pain upon himself because:

> True pain coming out of a man belongs primarily to God, it seems to me. I try and take it humbly to my heart, just as it is. I endeavour to make it mine, to live it. And I understand all the hidden meaning of the expression which has become hackneyed now: to commune with, because I really 'commune' with his [Delbende's] pain. (p. 64)

Some time later he learns that the doctor has died in a shooting accident and that suicide is suspected. He is distraught and seeks out his friend, the Curé de Torcy, who also knew Delbende. Torcy will not tolerate any talk of suicide: God alone will judge their dead friend. Torcy is a robust man, as efficient in running the affairs of his parish as his young colleague is ineffectual in Ambricourt. He sees the spirit of prayer in the curé d'Ambricourt but he, the pragmatist, realises that this will not help him to run his parish. He advises the young man to pray hard and to keep busy, not to allow people to use him, but to be firm. He might as well have told him to change the colour of his skin. The curé can work no harder than he is now labouring. His attempts at prayer often end up in *acidie*. The cancer in his stomach, of which he is unaware, prevents him from eating healthy food. He is forced to confine himself to a diet of bread and wine – symbols of the Eucharist. His appearance and erratic behaviour lead his parishioners to believe him to be an alcoholic. It suits them to so interpret his behavoiur. The Canon la Motte-Beuvron explains why:

> You see, my dear child, these people don't hate you for being simple, they're on their guard against it, that's all. Your simplicity is a kind of flame which scorches them. You go through the world with that lowly smile of yours as though you begged their pardon for being alive while all the time you carry a torch which you seem to mistake for a crozier. (pp. 145-6)

One person who is not on her guard against the parish priest is Chantal, the landlord's daughter. She has been made to suffer the infidelity of her father with the governess and the indifference of her mother, whose maternal instincts have been crushed by the premature death of her young son. Chantal has lost the innocence of youth and she seeks to test the curé at every opportunity. Talking about her father and the governess, she says:

> I heard them in the night. I was right under their window in the park. They don't even bother to draw the curtains now. (p. 103)

She is teasing him, searching for his prurience. She says that she plans to go to Paris, to 'disgrace' herself, in order to punish her parents. The curé, in a sudden moment of illumination, asks her for the letter in her bag. She is taken aback. 'You must be the devil,' (p. 106) she exclaims. There was indeed a letter, the contents of which are never revealed to us. Chantal meekly hands it over to him, realising that he can read minds. Despite her cruelty towards him, the curé bears her no ill will; rather he pities her. He sees that she is in revolt against God and the circumstances of her life.

> An unusual, almost alarming nobility bore witness to the power of evil, of sin, that sin which was not her own – God are we really such wretched creatures that a proud soul in revolt must needs turn against itself? (p. 107)

This priest, considered inept by the majority of his parishioners and superiors alike, attracts those who are suffering most. To the countess, in rebellion against a God who in her mind has taken her only son, he brings peace. Not before a struggle of significant proportions takes place, however. The countess believes that she is living a model Christian life. She goes to Mass and the sacraments – but with a heart of stone. Love, the most basic Christian virtue, has disappeared from her life: 'Hell is not to love anymore, madame,' (p. 127) the curé tells her. She slowly and painfully comes to realise that by rebelling against God's will she has endangered her eventual reunion with her dead son. For a long time she had been unable to recite the Lord's Prayer because of the words: 'Thy will be done.' By the end of their interview she has rediscovered peace and is able to accept God's will. After the curé's departure that night the countess dies, but not before writing him a note. We could easily, and with justification, claim that this episode is too pat, too contrived. It is a weakness in the technique of the plot. In the letter she says:

> I have lived in the most horrible solitude alone with the desperate memory of a child. And it seems to me that another child has brought me to life again. (p. 136)

All the priest can do is to reflect on the peace he has brought to another, while he himself continues to struggle. After the countess' death he is accused of spiritual blackmail, of having left the woman in a state of despair. He has no redress against these false accusations other than divulging the contents of the letter, which would mean his moral collapse. He remains silent, like Christ during his 'trial' by the high priests. Meanwhile, his health continues to deteriorate. It is as though he has taken the moral cancer at the heart of his parish upon himself, as though he is grappling with it like Christ with his father in Gethsemane. Sleepless nights, chronic stomach cramps, attacks on his character, all contribute to his earthly passion.

As he returns to the presbytery one evening he is overcome by a fit of violent coughing. He wakes up in a pool of his own blood; he stands up and faints again – the comparisons with the scourging and the road to Calvary are obvious. He is discovered by Seraphita, the young star of his catechism class who had betrayed him by saying, in front of her friends, that she had been attentive in class merely because he had 'beautiful eyes'.

Now it is she who nurses him, wipes his face clean. She acknowledges her fascination with him:

> 'It isn't that you're anythin' to look at', she muttered. 'It's just cause you're sad. You're sad even when you smile. I think that if I only knew why you was sad I shouldn't be wicked no more.' (p. 178)

Is this young girl supposed to represent Mary Magdalen or Veronica in modern dress? One could draw obvious parallels, but Bernanos' precise intention was unclear. What is clear, however, is that Seraphita's innocence has been destroyed. Exposed to evil at a very young age, she is the victim of presssures she cannot withstand. For it is difficult to be good when in youth you encounter evil everywhere, when 'ennui' has taken possession of the souls of your contemporaries. It is significant that she sees the good in the sick man, that she would like to be close to him, to find out the reasons for his sadness. Then she might not be wicked anymore. Good is emanating from him, God's grace, which she senses vaguely.

It is in Lille that the curé discovers the true nature of his illness, from an atheist doctor who is addicted to morphia and who is sentenced to die soon himself. The priest reproaches himself for not thinking of God when he first received the news:

> However hard I try now, I know I shall never understand by what terrible mischance I was able at such a time to forget the very name of God. I was alone, utterly alone, facing my death – and that death was a wiping out and nothing more. (p. 214)

His reaction is a human one, later to be spiritualised. The thought of death momentarily erased the joy of the resurrection

– Christ himself endured similar doubts. The curé's 'dark night of the soul' has now reached its crisis. Bernanos' spiritual convictions take over at the end of this man's life. In the apartment of his friend, Dufréty, a former priest, the curé's last words are: 'Does it matter? Grace is everywhere.' (p. 232) It is finished; his crucifixion is over. Grace has prevailed. The words quoted above are the crucial ones in the novel. Grace for the curé lies in the ability to love others more than self, to take their pain as his pain, to see suffering as proof of God's love. For it is by suffering that he has aligned himself with Christ. His life in the midst of a parish given over to evil shows how grace can win out, not in a spectacular fashion – that is not God's way – but in the transformation that can take place in an individual's soul, in the vision and insights that may appear only at special moments but that are none the less real for their elusiveness.

The Diary of a Country Priest was described by *The New York Times Book Review* as 'a novel of French village life which achieves a universal quality'. This universality is realised because Ambricourt is not merely a parish in France; it is the battlefield where the age-old struggle between good and evil continues unabated. The curé's life succeeds in convincing us that humility and love are at the core of all Christian behaviour and that suffering can pave the way to eternal joy. *The Diary* will always have a message for readers who are struggling in their own lives. Who among us would not share the curé's dying wish:

> Why worry, why look ahead? If I feel afraid I shall say: I am afraid, and not be ashamed of it. As soon as Our Lord appears before me may His eyes set me at rest. (pp. 228-9)

Christ himself sweated blood from fear. He died as a criminal, with shame as his comfort. Maybe Bernanos sometimes gives his spiritual convictions too free a rein in his writings; maybe he transposes some of his own convictions into the mouths of his characters. That said, however, his elucidation of the workings of grace in most uncongenial and unpromising situations has given us a novel whose power to stir the emotions to some sort of catharsis is as effective today as it was sixty odd years ago. There are flaws in the plot, especially with the obviousness of the overall message, but that does not detract seriously from the impact of one man, a clown for God, who lifted himself to heights of spirituality by his co-operation with grace, not in the traditional heroic manner of great saints but in the anti-heroic mode of the Bernanos genre. And in so lifting himself, he raised others to deflect their eyes from Mammon and look up for a glimpse of God. The curé was vindicated in death – in the quiet pondering of those whom he influenced. That was/is his epitaph and that's how Bernanos envisioned him in his study in novel form of the workings of grace.

NOTES

1. *Sous le soleil de Satan* (Plon/Livre de Poche, 1971), p. 25. The translation is my own.
2. Malcolm Scott, *The Struggle for the Soul of the French Novel. French Catholic and Realist Novelists 1850-1970* (London: Macmillan Press, 1989), p. 242.
3. *The Times* (London: 31 October 1978).
4. *The Diary of a Country Priest* (New York: Image Books, 1954), p. 2. All my references will be from this edition.
5. There are some graphic descriptions of how, as a young boy, he witnessed the alcoholism of his parents and of their customers in the family *bistrot*. His 'heredity' made him very wary of the dangers of alcohol. It is somewhat ironical that he will be suspected of overdrinking by his parishioners, who see this as the reason for his sickly appearance.

3

THE STRUGGLE BETWEEN THE SPIRIT AND THE FLESH IN JULIEN GREEN[1]

What is it about Julien Green (1900-98) that makes it so difficult to situate him in the French literary landscape? Is it the fact that he was born of American parents in Paris in 1900? Or is it because he was an Episcopalian who converted to Catholicism in his early teens? Or could it be the nostalgia he always felt for the American *Sud*, which his mother instilled in him from an early age with her stories about the American Civil War? Alternatively, it could be the result of the conflict that has always existed between Green's sexual preferences (he was a homosexual) and his deeply spiritual nature. He spanned the twentieth century, lived through two horrendous world wars, experienced the emergence of existentialist angst and the fear that God had abandoned his people. When reading Green's novels one is always conscious of how different they are from those of Bernanos and Mauriac, of whom he was a contemporary. This is not due merely to the fact that many of them are set in America but mainly because a strange atmosphere darkens his fictional universe, one similar to that found in Dostoevsky. His characters are victims of a pitiless destiny, fated to be frustrated in their quest for love and understanding. Similar to Dostoevsky's works, many of Green's characters can find no escape from their problems except through violence or madness. They are disturbing manifestations of the author's own obsessions. In his *Journal* he once wrote:

> I write out of an urgent need to forget, to plunge myself into a fictional world. And what do I find in this fictional world? My own problems which have been greatly heightened, to the point where they attain terrifying proportions.

What is most significant about these lines is the admission that Green's inner thoughts are best encapsulated in his fictional writings. He often made the point that his real *Journal* was to be found in his novels. He was a man whose life was full of paradoxes. An American who lived the vast majority of his life in Paris, he was never able to forget his Anglo-Saxon origins. A convert to Catholicism at the age of sixteen, he was unable to turn his back in a definitive manner on Protestantism. We will see that the Bible plays a major role in many of his protagonists' lives: they search it in the hope of finding some means of resolving their spiritual dilemmas. He was a deeply religious man who always found it difficult to reconcile the urgings of the flesh with the desire of the spirit to be pure. He was the first foreigner to be elected to the Académie Française and still his writings have not what you would call a distinctive French flavour. In his excellent study of Green's work, Michael O'Dwyer makes the point that Green has more in common with Hawthorne and Poe than he does with any French writer.[2] We would add the name of Graham Greene, another convert to Catholicism, to this list. The English novelist Greene has a fresh and controversial approach to Catholic dogma in his writings. Characters like Scobie *(The Heart of the Matter)* are forced to choose between performing charitable acts – which sometimes lead to sinful activity – and saving their souls. With Graham Green, we sometimes get the impression that sinners become saints – witness Scobie and the famous whiskey-priest in *The Power and the Glory*. Towards the latter half of Julien Green's work, a similar outlook is adopted.

Green's early life was happy and pure. His mother had a strong mistrust of the flesh as a result of the fact that her brother, Willie, died of syphilis, but also in part because of her puritan Protestant upbringing. She attempted to imbue her son with the same reservations about the body as she herself harboured. This led to an ambivalent attitude in the young boy. He had doubts about his soul, asking his mother on more than one occasion: 'Am I saved?'[3] In spite of his mother's reassurance that he had faith and was thus saved, the doubts persisted. His problems with his sexuality cannot have been helped either by the night his sister Mary, on observing him as a young boy (he was five years of age) with his hands in the forbidden area, called in his mother. The latter appeared, brandishing the bread knife and shouting: 'I'll cut it off!'[4] This fear of castration stayed with Green all his life, as did his mother's observation, on seeing him nude in the bath: 'Oh isn't it ugly!', referring to the same part of his body that she had threatened to remove forcibly. But for all these disturbing incidents, Green's early childhood was happy and his relationship with his mother very close. He possessed the same capacity of seeing the world through the eyes of a child as Frank McCourt does and the autobiography makes for compelling reading. The cruel ending of the innocence of youth by his colleagues in the *lycée* is described in terms of nostalgia and pathos. The world would never seem the same to Green: the lost paradise could never be reclaimed in this life.

To give the reader an opportunity to sample some of the qualities that make Green a marginal figure in French Christian letters, we will deal briefly with his first novel, *Mont-Cinère (Avarice House)*, which was published by Plon in 1926, and compare it to two of his later novels, *Moïra* (1950) and *Chaque homme dans sa nuit (Each Man in his Darkness*, 1960), which is widely considered to be a novel of conversion. A brief analysis will allow us to see the evolution that took place in Green's approach to spiritual matters between 1926 and 1960.

Avarice House is situated in America and its theme is miserliness. Mrs Fletcher, on the death of her husband, Stephen, is left with a daughter, Emily, whom she never really wanted, and the responsibility to run Avarice House on a purse string. However, her preoccupation with spending as little money as possible becomes an obsession. Every means of cutting down on expenses is exploited. She forces her teenage daughter to get rid of the maid and to take over many of her duties. She lights fires only when absolutely necessary. The cold interior of Avarice House symbolises the lack of love between the family members. The narrator notes the gulf that separates Mrs Fletcher from her daughter:

> She had never wanted the child, and had looked upon her as an intruder who only increased the household expenses; but her early animosity had at length given way to indifference.[5]

The arrival of Mrs Elliot, Mrs Fletcher's mother, heightens the tension. For this woman is more than a match for her daughter; she sees the extent to which her daughter sacrifices everything, even Emily's health and education, to her greed. Mrs Elliot and Emily become allies against Mrs Fletcher until a minor stroke renders the elderly lady an invalid. Emily becomes obsessed in her turn with the possessions of Avarice House and dreams of the day when it will all belong to her. She spies on her mother who, she suspects, is selling off items that would eventually form part of her inheritance. The novel is claustrophic in its stifling atmosphere. The women are on their guard against each other and are constantly on the lookout for signs of weakness. Religion is almost totally absent – the Fletchers rarely go to church. Like many of Green's characters, they are Protestants, but Protestants without faith. When the

Methodist minister of Glencoe, Mr Sedgwick, comes to visit Avarice House, Mrs Fletcher is greatly upset. The request that she make a contribution towards the upkeep of her church is strongly resisted. Emily is delighted to witness her mother's discomfiture and is fascinated at the same time with the middle-aged minister. She seeks to get close to him, writes him love letters that she subsequently tears up and slips into her Bible. Frustrated at every turn, deprived of love, Emily takes the drastic decision to marry Frank Stephens, a poor neighbour who has the merit, she believes, of being strong enough to impose his will on her mother. The plan falls asunder when she enters a room to hear Frank telling Laura, his daughter from his first marriage:

> All this belongs to us.... You and I are going to live here together all our lives, here in this house with all these fine things. (*Avarice House*, p. 354)

This is the final straw for the young heroine: she throws herself at her husband's young baby and grips it by the throat. Frank has to forcibly prevent her from strangling the child. Seeing all her hopes of love and understanding in ruins and realising that she will never be in full control of Avarice House, she sets it on fire and dies amidst the flames.

This first novel received a positive response from the French critics. It is a very dark account of hopeless desperation. Emily has no outlet for her positive desires. Abandoned at every turn by her mother, rejected by the minister, weakened by the death of her grandmother, she felt that she had no option but to turn to avarice and hate in order to attain some sort of revenge for a most unhappy existence. Roger Bichelberger makes the pertinent point that the greed which dominates the characters' lives in this novel is a reflection of the frustrated carnal desire that Green was experiencing at the time.[6] There is no outlet for love, all is trapped in a cold egoism. The fire that ravages the house at the end of the novel is the expression of a repressed passion. Emily seeks out God but sees around her numerous signs of his absence; she believes him to be indifferent to her plight. Her mother only prays when she feels threatened, like when there is a likelihood that she will have to pay out money for a doctor or for firewood. The gloomy atmosphere never lifts in this first period of Green's writings. In the other novels, which appear in the 1920s (*Adrienne Mesurat, Léviathan*), this despair is heightened. Green had not yet succeeded in reconciling his homosexuality and his religious convictions. With *Moïra*, we see the beginnings of some sort of resolution of the conflict between the spirit and the flesh.

Moïra is undoubtedly Green's finest novel. In it we have the superb description of how a young Protestant, Joseph Day, leaves his home in a remote mountain area to study in a unversity. The autobiographical elements are clear in this novel. Joseph's voyage of self-discovery is very similar to that of the young Green who went to study in the university of Virginia. Day is a religious fanatic who has very little in common with the activities or interests of the other students. He wishes to study Greek in order to read the Bible in the original, he sees sin at every turn and is particularly puritanical when it comes to sexual morality. Small wonder then that he is christened the 'Exterminating Angel' by another student, Killigrew. He is attracted to Praileau, an aloof figure with whom he quarrels when he feels the latter is poking fun at him about his red hair. The fight becomes very violent, as Joseph is unknowingly trying to purge the passion that fills his whole being: 'A sudden, mad joy filled him at his own strength and he felt some mysterious hunger in him being satisfied.'[7] Afterwards, Praileau makes the prophetic comment that there is a murderer lurking in Joseph.

Indeed, anyone who is as unaware of the passionate side of his nature as Joseph is, anyone as fanatical in his religious convictions, has to find an outlet for his tensions. He is attracted to Praileau but will not admit it to himself. When Moïra (in Greek, 'moïra' means destiny), the stepdaughter of his landlady, Mrs Dare, comes home on a visit, Joseph is forced to face up to his true character.

Killigrew told Joseph that the difference between him and the other students was that they gave in to their instincts. Joseph was quick to add: 'Their bestial instincts' (*Moïra*, p. 81). What Joseph fails to realise is that there is a beast lurking within each of us, which no amount of religious asceticism or denial will ever eradicate. He comes from a violent heredity; his father was blinded in a quarrel about his mother. He is also a very sensual person who feels so uncomfortable at sleeping in what had been Moïra's bed that he opts for the safety of the floor in order to avoid bad thoughts. David Laird, a quiet-spoken man who is studying to become a minister, is the one person to whom Joseph can speak freely. In an outburst that occurs shortly before his violent crime, he declares to David:

> Your love for God is peaceful, but I am mad for God. I can only love violently, because I am a passionate man. That is why I am more in danger of losing grace and why, in a way, I am nearer hell than you will ever be.
> (*Moïra*, p. 193)

He has attained some degree of self-knowledge at this point but he has yet to understand fully to what dangers his passionate nature exposes him. 'We shall burn, David, we shall burn in an eternity of joy' (*Moïra*, p. 194), he exclaims, hours before Moïra enters his room as part of a prank organised by Killigrew and MacAllister, who wish to see Joseph exposed to 'what the

Romans called lupa, a beast perpetually famished' (*Moïra*, p. 163). Joseph resists the advances of the she-wolf initially and it is only when, resigned to defeat, she is about to leave the room that he takes her in his arms: 'In the half-light she saw Joseph's eyes shining like the eyes of no other man she had ever seen, and she was suddenly filled with terror' (*Moïra*, p. 209).

After they make love, Joseph falls asleep. When he awakens to find the evidence of his sin beside him, he smothers Moïra. He cannot bear to look on this woman who has revealed the bestial side of his nature. As well as being a sinner, he now becomes a murderer. Extremes are what best characterise him. The dramatic treatment of the age-old struggle between the flesh and the spirit gives this novel a powerful force. There is much of Green in the character of Joseph. He too was the religious fanatic who wrote in the *Pamphlet contre les catholiques de France* in 1924:

> All Catholicism is suspect if it doesn't upturn the life of anyone practising it, if it doesn't mark him out in the eyes of the world, if it doesn't overwhelm him, if each day it doesn't make his life a renewed passion, if it isn't odious to the flesh, if it isn't unbearable.[8]

The *Pamphlet*, Green had subsequently admitted, was written by someone who was dejected at the thought that he would never be a saint. It contains all the ardour and fervour of the convert, the exigency of the zealot. In Praileau, also, we have the fictional representation of the great love of Green's life, Mark, whom he met while studying in Virginia. This love was never openly declared or physically consummated, just as Joseph will leave unsaid his true feelings towards Praileau. The optimistic note of the novel is found towards the end when Praileau offers to help Joseph to escape. The latter agrees to this proposal initially but later decides to return to face his punishment. He has been humbled by his experience and is in many ways a more attractive figure at the end of the novel than at the beginning. There is much optimism in the last lines, which describe Joseph moving to meet a stranger in the half-light. There are doubts with regard to the hero's destiny just as there are shadows on the street as he prepares to meet his fate.

Malcolm Scott maintains[9] that sexual attraction between two men constitutes the real theme of *Moïra*. It is obvious that Green found it difficult to speak of the problems that his struggle against his homosexual urges posed during his long life. *Le Malfaiteur* (1948) provided the first frank discussion of the subject in any of Green's fiction. However, when first published, the section entitled 'Jean's Confession' was missing. The novel doesn't hold together without this frank description of his homosexual adventures by the young hero, who wishes to warn his female friend, Hedwige, that the man with whom she has fallen in love is one of his former lovers. It was necessary to wait for the 1973 Pléiade edition for the 'Confession' to be published. It is a moving plea for more understanding in relation to homosexuality:

> The most wrenching punishment that can befall an individual whose sexual orientation causes his banishment from society is that he be reduced to pretence or to making a major scene. And if he doesn't have the heart to declare himself, he is unjustly obliged to live like a hypocrite.[10]

Green's personal dilemma is described in the lines above. Should he openly declare his preferences and be exposed to the incomprehension and ridicule of the public? Or make a big scene, live like a hypocrite? We know from his *Pamphlet* what he thought of hypocrisy. Green didn't really come up with any solution to this dilemma, other than to live in a chaste manner for vitually all of his adult life. While the pain and suffering did not lessen with the passing of the years, being able to discuss the problem openly with his readers did have some positive results, as we shall now see.

Each Man in his Darkness (1960) introduces us to the charismatic figure of Wilfred Ingram, a devout Catholic who is also a womaniser. Once more, the novel is set in America, but it is a more modern setting than either *Avarice House*, which is Dickensian in its atmosphere, or *Moïra*. Wilfred, though a sinner, is more evangelical than Joseph Day. People who come in contact with him sense a spiritual dimension that they envy. The hero knows how far removed he is from the image people have created of him and he would feel far freer were he not so aware of the sinfulness of his nature. There is a powerful scene at the beginning of the novel when he goes to see his dissolute uncle, Horace, who, like Wilfred, is a Catholic who has sinned a lot. Wilfred observes with fear this replica of himself who is preparing to die. The old man needs reassurance but his nephew feels inadequate to the task: 'I cannot cure you', Wilfred exclaims, 'It would take a saint to do that and I'm not a saint.'[11] Despite his protests his uncle retorts: 'Yes, you are!…. Right now you're like a saint. We all are at one moment or another of our lives' (*Each Man in his Darkness*, p. 64).

The question of whether or not Wilfred is a saint is a delicate one. Is Graham Greene's whiskey-priest a saint? He too has sinned a great deal but possesses enough humility to accept his faults and deeply regret them. Julien Green gives us a glimpse, in the character of Wilfred, of a man who attains a degree of conversion through his suffering. He is plagued with guilt:

> He kept a rosary in his pocket, but when he went to town to misbehave he always left it at home in a drawer, so that the little crucifix saw nothing. (*Each Man in his Darkness*, p. 44)

But his awareness of sin does not prevent him from engaging in illicit sexual activity. He makes love to women, confesses his sins and then resumes his philandering. His real predicament occurs when he meets a distant cousin, Phoebé, with whom he falls in love. Many obstacles are placed in his path. The first one is the fact that she is married, and so he risks not only his own soul, but also hers, if they consummate their passion. And then there is her purity, of which James Knight, her husband, points out to Wilfred:

> There's something untouched in her. She is undefiled. Sin would make her lose it, but sin is unknown to her. She is not like us. If there's someone in the world I believe in, it's she. (*Each Man in his Darkness*, p. 288)

Wilfred realises that he is gambling his own and her salvation because Phoebé's love for him is deep and unconditional. To abuse this, he believes, would be to sin greviously. And yet he cannot give her up. Enter Max, a strange character who follows Wilfred home from the church one day and speaks to him about religion.[12] Max is attracted to Wilfred and frustrated by the latter's insensibility to his sexual advances.[13] In a moment of desperation, Wilfred goes to visit his disturbed friend and is shot by him. The hero's final gesture is to forgive Max – the ultimate Christian gesture. His drama thus seems to reach a peaceful resolution, which is highly unusual in Green. James Knight is convinced that Wilfred has entered a type of mystical peace. He notes that never has he seen such 'an expression of happiness on any face as that which lit up Wilfred's'. And he adds: '…he was watching us from afar, from a region of light' (*Each Man in his Darkness*, p. 346).

Clearly there is an optimistic attitude to sin, salvation and death that is new in Green. Wilfred, a sinner, is saved. The pessimism of his first novel, the violence of *Moïra*, have given way to a hopeful climax. Wilfred ends up by experiencing first hand the peace he was unconsciously instrumental in securing for his uncle Horace. His goodness finally overcomes his lustfulness.

So what has this brief sketch of Green's writings revealed? Obviously the evolution from *Avarice House* to *Each Man in his Darkness* has been significant. Gone are the despair and the doubts, the inability to escape from an implacable destiny. The God we encounter in the latter novel is a much more forgiving and proactive force than in *Avarice House*. He is also far more present to his creatures, more caring about their destiny. *Moïra* has the force and passion of a Shakespearian tragedy, with its hero, Joseph Day, setting in motion the train of events that will lead to his downfall. It has positive moments but the conclusion is shrouded in the darkness as he walks towards his unknown destiny. *Each Man in his Darkness* has an obvious optimism in its very title.[14]

Why do we assert that Green is a marginal figure in French Christian letters? The fact that he was elected to the Académie Française – he filled the seat formerly occupied by Mauriac – would indicate that he is highly regarded by the literary establishment in France. His works appear in several tomes in the Pléiade series and so he can hardly be considered marginal in literary terms. No, his marginality has to do with the nature of his themes and the atmosphere that dominates his novels. Green's work is at times a denunciation of the world and of existence – it announces the theme of 'nausea' so prevalent in

Sartre. Exile, solitude, suffocation, suffering are all to be seen in the novels of this American who was brought up in France, in this convert to Catholicism who was plagued by his unworthiness in the face of God. For anyone with an interest in the links between literature and spirituality, Julien Green is an indispensable reference. His life and his works are studies of the perennial struggle between good and evil, between grace and free will, which preoccupies the mind of every thinking individual. In addition, Green had to try to come to terms with his homosexuality, which was at war with his innate yearning for purity. Through his writings Green explores the depths of his sinfulness and eventually he seems to find acceptance of his duality. Shortly after his death, the President of the Société Internationale d'Etudes Greeniennes, Michèle Raclot, wrote:

> Julien Green's faith underwent numerous fluctuations at certain periods during his life, but it was so deeply ingrained in him that he couldn't, any more than his hero, Wilfred, cheapen it in order to avoid spiritual obstacles.[15]

His struggles ended on 13 August 1998. Only then did he come to know the answers that plagued him during his life. For his readers, Green remains present in his books, which I recommend you read and re-read in order to be more receptive to the secrets contained within them.

NOTES

1. I deal with the influence of Green on John Broderick in the second half of the book.

2. Michael O'Dwyer, *Julien Green. A Critical Study* (Dublin: Four Courts Press, 1997). There is an obvious rich vein to be mined in the similarities between Green and these two American writers but it will not be our preoccupation in this chapter.

3. *Partir avant le jour,* in *Jeunes Années Autobiographie I* (Paris: Seuil/Points, 1984), p. 28.

4. Ibid., p. 21.

5. *Avarice House.* Translated from the French by Marshall Best (London: Quartet Books, 1991), p. 70.

6. Roger Bichelberger, *Julien Green ou le combat avec Dieu* (Doctoral Thesis, University of Metz, 1978), p. 99.

7. *Moïra.* Translated from the French by Denise Folliot (Quartet Books, 1985), p. 27.

8. *Pamphlet contre les catholiques de France* (Plon, 1924), p. 68.

9. M. Scott, *The Struggle for the Soul of The French Novel* (London: MacMillan Press, 1989).

10. *Le Malfaiteur* (Fayard/Livre de Poche, 1955), p. 141.

11. *Each Man in his Darkness.* Translated by Anne Green (Quartet Books, 1990), p. 63.

12. In an excellent paper he delivered on this novel in the Sorbonne in 1995, Pierre Masson wondered how realistic it was that in a novel published in 1960 and bearing all the hallmarks of modern civilisation, religious issues should be so omnipresent. He notes: 'In the setting of large department stores, snack-bars, in cars and buses, it appears as though the only preoccupation of human beings is the difficulty of choosing between Catholicism and Protestantism in order to ensure the eternal salvation of their souls' (Pierre Masson, 'De l'insolite au surnaturel dans Chaque homme dans sa nuit', in *Julien Green et l'Insolite*, Société Internationale d'Etudes Greeniennes, 1998, p. 111). He adds how bizarre it appears to him that complete strangers should, on their first meeting, immediately strike up a conversation about religion.

13. 'Between the two, and for weeks, since the moment they met, their tacit dialogue was each time resumed, no matter what their lips said. Max was willing and Wilfred was not. Max wanted to kill Wilfred for that reason' (*Each Man*, p. 335).

14. Critics like Michael O'Dwyer note the importance of the unfinished title of the novel: 'Each man in his darkness goes towards his light.' This conveys a positive message to the reader.

15. *Hommage à Julien Green: 6 septembre 1900 – 13 août 1998*, SIEG, September 1998, p. 4.

4

JEAN SULIVAN:
A MARGINAL WRITER

Jean Sulivan (1913-80) is not as well known in France as his talent deserves. He is even less familiar to an Irish audience, in spite of the active Sulivan school that has been nurtured in NUI Galway by Professor Padraig O'Gormaile of the French faculty. Sulivan's real name was Joseph Lemarchand and he was born in the small Breton village of Montauban in 1913. He adopted the *nom de plume* Jean Sulivan after watching Preston Sturges' Hollywood comedy, *Sullivan's Travels*. In this film, the hero, having become disillusioned with life as a Hollywood director, travels around America in an effort to find an authentic mode of existence. At the end of the film, he returns to Hollywood a stronger and more determined character. Sulivan had a great interest in cinema. Journeys (be they geographical displacements or spiritual odysseys, or both) are commonplace in his works, and his characters frequently set off to foreign countries such as Africa, the US, India, Italy, Switzerland. The pseudonym he chose is thus revealing about Sulivan's main preoccupations as a writer. Like Sturges' hero, he never allowed himself to remain immobile and constantly sought out new challenges and experiences. He is constant in his restless search for the inner secret of life, the Truth, knowing that he will never find it.

Sulivan suffered pain and loss as a child: his father was killed on the front in Argonne in 1916, which left his mother with no other option than to remarry if she wished to hold on to her small farm. Like Baudelaire before him, Sulivan was inconsolable at the prospect of a stranger coming between himself and his mother. In the autobiographical account of his mother's death, *Devance tout adieu* (1966), he wrote:

> My mother is remarrying. That child must be experiencing fear, shame and emptiness.[1]

There was more than a little anger also. Apart from the trauma associated with the remarriage, Sulivan's childhood was typical of that period in rural France: he worked on the farm, attended religious ceremonies and began formal education. His mother was a devout Catholic and on a daily basis she read passages of the Gospel aloud to her son, who became very attached to its 'breath' and 'rhythm' – the music of the sounds intrigued him initially; the depth of meaning came later. As a writer, he later sought to revitalise the Word by being provocative and enigmatic, by forcing the reader to make up his/her mind about what was hidden in the text. He wasn't a believer in supplying ready-made answers or value-judgements.

When he decided to enter the *'petit séminaire'* in 1926, it may have been out of a desire to escape from a poor background and to gain entry into a world of ecclesiastical power and influence, as well as on account of his spiritual convictions – his mother's unflinching faith was a major impact. He was ordained priest in Rennes in 1938 but he later described his years in the seminary as a 'purgatory'. His rebellious nature would not allow him to accept blindly the rhetoric and conditioning that were an integral part of the priest's training in the twenties and thirties in France and elsewhere.

After ordination, he was sent to teach in the Catholic *lycée* in Rennes and he was also Chaplain at the local university. His next twenty years were divided between pastoral and cultural commitments; and this partly explains why his first novel, *Le Voyage intérieur*, was not published by Gallimard until 1958, when he was forty-five. In between, he became well known in cultural circles in Rennes: he ran a cinéclub, *La Chambre Noire*, and a highly successful cultural centre, *Renaissance spirituelle*, which had thinkers of the calibre of François Mauriac (then at the height of his powers), Gabriel Marcel (the father of Christian existentialism), le père Daniélou (the future Cardinal), and Emmanuel Mounier (the founder of *Esprit*), as guest-speakers. He also founded a monthly newspaper, *Dialogues-Ouest*, which enjoyed much success and to which Sulivan contributed articles and editorials. All this was by way of preparation. At the end of the 1950s, his bishop, the future Cardinal Roques, allowed Sulivan the freedom from his pastoral duties to embark on a literary career. The bishop saw the moral and social value in having a member of the diocesan clergy engaged in such writing. This was a daring decision as he knew how Sulivan viewed the role of the priest-writer. This man was not going to be an apologist for the Catholic religion and had no intention of constructing a pietistic picture of the Church. Sulivan was aware that he was writing at a time when the old Catholic order in France was giving way to a new underground, marginal religion. There was the highly significant advent of the worker-priests, later to be banned, and Vatican II, with its many changes in the liturgy and religious practice in general, provoked much upheaval for many sincere Catholics. Young people in particular were disenchanted with many of the Church's teachings and some were choosing to live in communities where they hoped a more fulfilling spiritual life could be realised. Hippies, student revolts, drugs, were very characteristic of the sixties throughout the world.

Sulivan is very much a writer of this time, a time of questioning and revolt against traditional values. It is significant that many of his agnostic and atheistic characters are more attractive and possess more genuinely Christian qualities than those who claim membership of the Church. In the brief sketch of his life up to his 'rebirth' – the word is his, not mine – through literature in 1958, we can see the non-conformist, wounded, marginal nature of the man, Joseph Lemarchand, who was to become in his turn the marginal writer, Jean Sulivan.

It is impossible to separate literary from spiritual sources in the writings of Sulivan. Each time you pick up one of his novels or essays you notice how these two elements are interwoven. For Sulivan, literature and spirituality, poetry and faith, are part of the same mystique. In this chapter, I propose to treat Sulivan as a marginal writer. You see, marginality is the key to understanding the essence of Sulivan's thinking and writings. He is situated on the fringes of French literature because he doesn't belong to any school or grouping. He is not acknowledged by, nor did he seek the approval of, the literary establishment. By the term 'marginal writer' I mean an author who deliberately distances himself from the conventional style of language, plot and characterisation. He isn't primarily concerned with literary niceties but remains attached to the aesthetic side of writing. He is, after all, a writer whose tools are words and who is a very skilled wordsmith. He is acutely aware of the musicality of language, of its symbolic and poetic powers, of its rhythm and breath. However, at a definitive stage in his literary development Jean Sulivan turns away from traditional notions of a literature that seeks critical acclaim and absorbs aesthetic beauty; he pushes his words to the margins of literature, even to the limits of coherence. He is suspicious of the success-syndrome that might betray his interior truth:

> It is difficult to speak without a mask. In order to reach
> the specialists, whose souls have often been spoiled by

reading too much, and yet without whom you reach nobody, you have to dress things up. That is to say you must express things in a certain way, transform the most private truth into a literary truth.[2]

According to Sulivan, the 'most private truth' paradoxically cannot, without much pain, become a 'literary truth'. He refuses to compromise. Everything is a struggle for him, a struggle between the Word[3] and its antithesis, lies, also between artifice and authenticity. Elusiveness in the use of language and forms is, in Sulivan, a key to the mystery of life itself.

His literary beginnings date from the end of the 1950s, at a time when France had endured the horror of two world wars and when the absurdity of the human condition appeared obvious to thinking people. The New Novel, with its fragmented style and absence of organic development of character, was gaining popularity. Catholic literature, which had enjoyed such success in France at the end of the nineteenth and the beginning of the twentieth century, began to falter because its masters – Claudel, Péguy, Bloy, Barbey d'Aurevilly, Mauriac, Bernanos – had not been equalled by their successors. As the critic Joseph Majault observed:

> Now that they have gone, many feel that the last generation of those who brilliantly represented the alliance of literature and religion has disappeared with them. None of their successors has acquired either their authority or their readership, and what was called Catholic literature now seems no more than a remnant from a distant past.[4]

In *Petite littérature individuelle*, Sulivan notes that the spiritual and intellectual atmosphere of the second half of the twentieth century demanded a new approach on the part of a novelist of Christian inspiration such as himself. He realised how futile the efforts of the minor writers of the fifties and sixties were because they were trying to emulate the great Catholic novelists who had preceded them:

> But whether it is that genius cannot be imitated, because former cultural and religious signs have become outdated, they can only communicate with a public living in the past. Spiritual heirs are either out of touch or else forced to renew themselves and follow a new direction, or else indeed to return to silence.[5]

He is seeking something different, to invent another way of presenting spirituality. It would be inaccurate to maintain that Catholic literature had no more readers in the France of the fifties and sixties. However, Sulivan saw the stupidity of imitating the great predecessors when their era had passed: 'It is in invention that the future of Christian writers lies if they want to be something other than specialists, scribes or efficient instruments on the market of religion', he wrote again in *Petite littérature individuelle*.[6] As distinct from minor Catholic writers like Luc Estang or Jean Montaurier, who were trying to prolong a dated style of presentation, Sulivan wanted a fresh vision. This had not always been his search. His first novels contained nothing to surprise those who were used to accepted plot-designs and traditional character formation. This form of his writing reached its apex with *Mais il y a la mer*, published in 1964, which earned for him the *Grand Prix catholique de littérature*. His description of the awards' ceremony shows how much this ritual with its rites and customs embarrassed him. He was convinced that he had betrayed something:

> The journalists surround him, place a book in his hand that he is to hold like that on his chest. 'Turn around. Face this way please!' He must look like a bewildered boy just after making his First Communion. What a poor excuse for a rebel![7]

Why did he accept this prize if it caused him so much discomfort? His first reason was to please his mother, who was impressed the following day, while reading *La Croix*, to see her son acknowledged by the Catholic press. In addition, there had been the efforts of Daniel-Rops, soon to die, who had supported Sulivan to win this honour. The latter explains, on seeing his embarrassment, that at least now he will be read. Sulivan was not convinced, however. He was very ill-at-ease in this milieu where everyone knew everyone else and offered each other compliments: this smacked of inauthenticity, croneyism and imposture. His reaction to the success of *Mais il y a la mer* has always struck me as excessive, because it is a beautiful novel, probably the most powerful Sulivan has written, and in no place does one detect an edifying tone likely to impress respectable Catholic opinion. The hero, Cardinal Ramon Rimaz, discovers, or rediscovers, late in life that he has deserted his first vocation, that of serving the poor, to become a notable, a member of the social and ecclesiastical hierarchy. His final gesture is to take the place of a political prisoner, whom he has regularly visited. The prisoner escapes dressed in the cardinal's robes, and the latter thus becomes the object of the persecution and disdain of the political authorities with whom he had been so friendly during his active ministry. Now he has to endure the fate of the meek, the poor, the marginals of this world, with whom he wishes once more to identify. *Mais il y a la mer* won a prestigious prize, which proves that it corresponds to a traditional conception of literature, but Sulivan was not happy. He wrote later in *Devance tout adieu*:

> Impostor! You describe a cardinal who renounces his
> purple garb, all the external signs of glory, while you, the
> author, the creator of this cardinal yet to be born, dare
> show yourself in public to lap up all this praise.[8]

And yet Cardinal Rimaz is the model of embraced
marginality which becomes manifest in much of his later
output. In addition, the self-flagellation was unnecessary as he
had produced and honed a literary work of rare beauty. Did
Sulivan err in turning his back on such a brilliant start to his
writing career? We will never know. All we do know is that
when he faced towards the deserts of marginality, he created a
new mode of expression. Thus, after *Mais il y a la mer*, Sulivan
moved away from a form of literature that concerned itself
primarily with favourable criticism and sales. The classical NRF
(*Nouvelle Revue Française* – a prestigious French journal in
which all the major French writers appear) style became
fragmented, jerky, and suddenly one has difficulty
differentiating between the narrator, the author and the
characters. Listen to these lines taken from *D'amour et de mort
à Mogador* (1970):

> I like to see the puppets, but also the puppeteer, his
> hands, the strings that control the puppets, just as I like
> to contemplate the narrator who leads his characters,
> identifies with or separates himself from them. And you,
> the scribe who leads the narrator, who exactly pulls your
> strings?[9]

Any author can pull the puppets' strings but Sulivan pulled
willy-nilly until they and their viewers (in this case, the readers)
became confused about the meaning and purpose of their
movements. He moved quickly to the margins of the written
word, where time, plot, character and language are deliberately

convoluted. In the novel just mentioned it is difficult to know with whom or what we are dealing. It's as though the objectivity of the novelist is being called into question. The reader ends up realising that what is important is communication between Sulivan and him/her. That communication is dependent on one being sensitive to the breath and poetry of this writing, being capable of listening to the sounds and absorbing them. Because Sulivan is no longer trying to create a logical narrative but simply to give us seemingly unconnected news about his characters. Many of them are based on real people and we encounter them in various works. These characters are at variance with any system that reduces an individual's independence. We meet drug-addicts, prostitutes, tramps, priests who rebel against the establishment, homosexuals, all victims of social and religious discrimination. Note that for many of these characters, their marginality is voluntary and is not an imposed choice. That is important – they are willing victims. Witness the hero, or anti-hero, of *Les mots à la gorge* (1969), Daniel Dorme, a journalist who finds himself one day at a crossroads in his existence. He takes a decision that completely changes his life. He leaves his job, his wife and daughter, his financial security, in order to become a tramp. He wanders around the streets of the city 'in glorious dishonour'[10] because he is no longer prostituting himself to social propriety. He is no longer conforming to the conventional image people had of him. Stripped of his worldly goods, of traditional comforts, Dorme remarks on the futility of the business world, where people are preoccupied with the acquisition of money at any cost. This Sulivanian hero knows that he is the privileged one, he who has nothing, he who has been 'chosen' in a way. We read: 'Everything has fallen on top of me, everything has taken place without my being able to control it. I have become a happy fool.'[11] He is free.

Sulivan is attached to this type of witness. The more we progress through his work, the more we see that plot is less and less important and that the language is heading more and more towards its ultimate limit: silence. But this silence is an expressive silence, an eloquent silence. What we hold on to especially, after we have finished reading one of his novels, is this strange family of characters: Strozzi, Paul Esteban, Daniel Dorme, Minka, Jude, a whole array of people who express things that we have been thinking ourselves for a long time. They resemble old friends who drag us towards a strange yet familiar country. This race of people, which had Sulivan's preference, resemble their creator also through their spiritual odyssey. Fraternity, communal life, authenticity, interior illumination, rebirth, uprooting, wounds, this is the type of vocabulary that Sulivan employs to describe their experiences. One word summarises their lot: marginality. For Sulivan, the marginal is someone who has undergone a moment of intense interior revelation, which gives him a keener insight into existence. Marginality is thus a lot more than a mere sociological phenomenon. Sulivan doesn't seek to change the structures of society, to become the champion of the poor, of the victims of injustice – he is not an Abbé Pierre who wrote novels. Marginality does not impoverish but rather enriches those who embrace it, by helping them to see that their present life is without meaning, that it is false, artificial. One day they begin to live, to look around them, to breathe anew. It's as if they have just seen the truth about existence. The process resembles what happens to Paul on the road to Damascus when he received a flash of insight into his life. In *Matinales II*, which outlines his spiritual itinerary, Sulivan explains:

> I would like first of all to talk about a race of men. This
> is how I see them: unable to judge anyone, respectful of

people's differences, and yet in possession of an implacable capacity for unearthing plots. They are always attentive to read on people's lips other words than those that are pronounced…. They're all the more in love with the world for the fact that they walk in the shade. They are inattentive to prestige and their life is an insult to all power, even though they have no problem saluting Princes. They're not fond of obedience, even less so of commanding. The feeling of ridicule would always prevent them from falling into that particular trap.[12]

Sulivan's 'family' can be found among those who have been wounded, marginalised, exiled by life, and yet who come to know an indiscernible happiness when they are capable of looking at their lives lucidly. They are forced to live in a contemporary world which has tried to erase all signs of God's existence, but offering nothing that might satisfy the thirst for transcendence which is a human necessity. Liberated from restraints imposed by social conventions, by the need to earn money in order to live and to support a family, Sulivan's characters happen on hope in the midst of all the deserts of human defeat.

So Sulivan proposes a quest to his readers as well as to himself, this quest that will only conclude after death and that is everywhere in his writings. His life was full of significant turning points – in particular the death of his mother and his trip to India, where he visited the French Benedictine, Henri le Saux[13] – but the search for the holy grail never ceased to inspire him. It was this quest that gave meaning to his life. Marginality was his way of living out the quest. Always on the move towards something new, he knew that real death occurred when a person remains motionless, when s/he stops searching and so stops breathing in a meaningful way. In this way, literature also had to look for something else, in order to capture more efficiently profound interior experiences. Sulivan refused to become part of any accepted category of writers, to please readers who were only seeking entertainment in literature. We read in *Joie errante* this challenge to his readers:

> Your anxiety moves me. All these comings-and-goings in space and time…. You would like an accomplished book which would grab you by the throat! I don't want to lie to this extent. Why should I allow myself to be carried along by the mechanics of a plot?…. Why should I extend for you this trap, while I'd hide behind the smooth rampart of literature, totally unblemished, watching you look at yourselves, delighted with my posturing?[14]

There are times when Sulivan displays much distrust of literature, or at least a suspicion with regard to a certain interpretation of literature that tries to present a clear image of a world in crisis. He knows he has a slightly paradoxical attitude because he provokes his readers by abandoning a detached, objective form of narration, well-constructed characters and classical story-lines. He doesn't seek to produce 'beautiful' books, to 'polish' or embellish, to become a notable. Another need develops in him, that of sharing with his readers a strange spiritual experience that changes everything. Afterwards, an interior language breaks the logical sequence and the author expresses himself on a totally different level. Joseph Majault wrote:

> The reader is no longer subjected to a logical outcome, but rather to short, obscure, broken sequences where time and situations are fragmented. At one and the same

> time broken and maintained, your attention obeys
> suggestive powers, jumps from one page to the next while
> waiting for a conclusion which escapes, which is sketched
> but not defined. This void pushes the reader to stand in
> for the narrator in order to give an ending to a text that
> is left deliberately unfinished.[15]

Sulivan is disturbing, annoying, paradoxical, but not illogical at a deeper level of reading, as M. Majault points out. In order to grasp the Sulivanian challenge, the readers must give of themselves so that the work can find its conclusion in them. As in the parables, every solution remains deliberately vague. Sulivan only gives enigmatic answers to the questions that his characters and, by extension, we ourselves have to face. We wonder at the end of a story what is going to happen afterwards. In a sense, all Sulivan is doing is enunciating the Word in his way, with all its cries for interior upheaval, its paradoxes and its poetry. The poem that gives meaning to life – this is what inspires Sulivan's writing and what makes him so original. He saw all his writings as one great poem. In his view, the poetic function of art can reveal the spiritual meaning of things, by extracting from the apparent chaos, from the unfathomable absence, a harmonious image of the world. The symbolic can thus render visible the invisible, by going from disorder to order, from emptiness to fullness, from the unformed to the formed. He sees the writer as a wanderer, someone who must uproot himself, depart, 'refuse the words of the tribe', as he himself once said. Instead of being presented as an object, Sulivan's oeuvre is proposed as a call, as a language that must germinate within the reader, like poetry, like the Gospel, the ultimate Word. Henri Guillemin, literary critic and friend of Sulivan, sensed his prophetic quality:

Sulivan seems to write for a world to come, already present in the underground, as if the Word has scarcely begun to be heard, as if it had its whole future ahead of it. He thus sketches a new aspect of a faith which is at odds with Western regionalism and which alone is capable of rejoining the main anthropological current and living up in a true sense to its name.[16]

Indeed, the Word may have bypassed the Western world and taken up its abode in the Third World and in parts of the East, where famine and disease are more favourable to the meaning of the Word than the selfishness and materialism of Western lifestyles. Guillemin is also correct when he talks of Sulivan's 'liberating voice', this voice that forces us to lead our own quest beyond the parable-text, to find our own answers to the dilemmas posed by existence. Sulivan provides the bridge between Catholic literature and what Joseph Majault has referred to as 'literature of Christian inspiration',[17] which appeared in France towards the end of the 1950s. He doesn't feel obliged to defend the Catholic Church against the forces of science and republicanism, as Bernanos and, to a lesser extent, Mauriac, did. No, he simply states that one must know oneself as intimately as possible and in this way come to a better understanding of God. He was not interested in literary celebrity status, in social or ecclesiastical advancement, but rather in inciting his readers towards spiritual renaissance. These lines capture his basic ideas on literature:

> The books which count are an invitation to live above ourselves and our mediocrity. Anything that merely relates, explains, or even more so, denigrates, is insignificant. I invite you therefore to search for real books, which spring from an authentic experience, that are written with blood, joy and pain.[18]

No simplicity there, no casual reading, no answered questions – only the continuous search. Writing involves a catharsis for Sulivan, for his characters and for the readers who can embark on an unending quest which is full of mystery and enigmas. The search is everything; marginality is a way of living out the quest. Whenever Sulivan feels he has achieved something, he immediately turns his back on it and searches for something new. The form of his writing reflects the restlessness of his spirit. The clarity, coherence and free-flowing elegance of *Mais il y a la mer* (1964) develop into the ellipsis, non-sequential, enigmatic, mal-punctuated prose of his final works, especially *Joie errante (Wandering Joy,* 1970), which, as its title might suggest, is very Eckhartian in theme. He possesses a prophetic voice that will continue to attract many more readers in France and elsewhere, particularly among those who do not automatically embrace accepted standards and who, like Sulivan and his characters, are prepared to take risks, to live out the moment, to be receptive to the Word and the challenges it poses. Sulivan died in 1980, shortly after being the victim of a hit-and-run accident as he was coming out of the Bois de Boulogne on one of his interminable walks. He has not yet assumed a high profile in French literary circles but more and more articles are now being published on his work and English translations of his novels and essays are also appearing. It should be remembered that he comes on the literary scene in France at a time when no one really expected a strong spiritual witness to emerge – 1958 was, after all, a time of spiritual anguish and existential despair and the vast majority of writers reflected this depressing ambience. The fact that Sulivan wrote in such an unconventional manner about such unconventional characters probably added to the tendency to steer clear of him. You should not expect a strong story-line in his novels, a classical third-person narration, or a linear sequence of events. His strengths are as much spiritual as they are literary – which is not to say that he doesn't possess many literary gifts. Indeed, his prose in places is as pure as you'll find. What you get out of reading him is dependent on your openness to his paradoxical approach and your preparedness to enter into the 'breath', rhythm and poetry that are integral elements of his style. Let me conclude with Sulivan's own explanation of why he is fascinated with marginals of all sorts and with the concept of marginality in general:

> I don't believe that I write because of the need to share secrets. I prefer to tell stories, to give emphasis to a narrator and some characters while I watch from backstage. My personal journal is mixed in with my books. My preference would be to speak neither about faith nor about myself, but of men and women who set out against the night, of highways and skyscrapers, of the rejects of society, of love, its wounds and cures, in the secret hope that the absolute would offer a sign in spite of me. But many readers, including believers, have written to say that my books have helped them to go on living. It is for them that I am writing this.[19]

With the witness he provides, I think it likely that Sulivan will continue for many years to help people, especially those who suffer or are wounded in any way, 'to go on living'. That is no small role for a writer.

NOTES

1. *Devance tout adieu* (Paris: Gallimard, 1966), p. 90.
2. Ibid., p. 140.
3. A key word in his writings is Word, which recurs with intriguing

frequency. It goes back to the opening lines of John's Gospel where he says: 'In the beginning was the Word.' It would take someone far better versed in theology than I to analyse the secret of the Word, which is, in any case, a mystery. I would merely suggest that we see it as Sulivan saw it. He was never a man for simplistic analyses: he loved portmanteau words with a tantalising range of interpretations. But the Word for him is the Word of all words, the ultimate Word. Without a basic understanding of the mystique and indeed mystery of the Word, much of the significance of Sulivan's writings will be lost on the reader.

4. Joseph Majault, *L'évidence et le mystère* (Paris: Le Centurion, 1978).

5. *Petite littérature individuelle* (Paris: Gallimard, 1971), p. 142.

6. Ibid., p. 131.

7. *Devance tout adieu*, op. cit., p. 153.

8. Ibid., pp. 153-4.

9. *D'amour et de mort à Mogador* (Paris: Gallimard, 1970), p. 18.

10. *Les mots à la gorge* (Paris: Gallimard, 1969), p. 14.

11. Ibid., p. 237.

12. Matinales II. *La traversée des illusions* (Paris: Gallimard, 1976), p. 83.

13. The trip to India is described in *Le Plus Petit Abîme* (Paris: Gallimard, 1969). His step-brother, Maurice Récan, who went to collect Sulivan at the airport on his return from India, almost didn't recognise him. He stated in an interview: 'He was like a different man.' It is clear from his account that Sulivan underwent a type of spiritual conversion in the ashram run by Le Saux on the banks of the river Cavery.

14. *Joie errante* (Paris: Gallimard, 1974), p. 147.

15. J. Majault, *L'évidence et le mystère*, pp. 176-7.

16. H. Guillemin, *Sulivan ou la parole libératrice* (Paris: Gallimard, 1977), p. 56.

17. *L'évidence et le mystère*, op. cit.

18. Bloc-Notes, *Editions SOS* (1986), pp. 45-6.

19. *Morning Light* (trans) Joseph Cunneen and Patrick Gormally (New York: Paulist Press, 1988), p. 27.

5

ALBERT CAMUS: AN EXISTENTIALIST WRITER WITH A SENSE OF THE ABSOLUTE

Albert Camus (1913-60) is generally regarded as one of the brightest stars in twentieth-century French letters. He became unpopular in his own time among his erstwhile Communist allies for his outspoken comments on totalitarian regimes, but people are now beginning to see how courageous a stand he took in denouncing what he saw as the excesses of Soviet expansionism. His existentialist contemporary, Sartre, did not engage in the politics of Stalin-denunciation because he would lose many of his supporters. Bryan Appleyard, in a thoughtful article on Camus entitled 'The Lone Voice of Sanity'[1], noted wistfully that it was Sartre who came to dominate French intellectual life in the forties and fifties, while Camus was ostracised. After structuralism came post-structuralism and deconstruction, ideologies that changed the whole face of literary appreciation and criticism in France and elsewhere. Form became everything; 'isms' held sway in a remarkable fashion. Mr Appleyard analyses the fruits of this:

> Hypnotised by these complex, radical and frequently incomprehensible systems, students and teachers turned against the humane, moral impulses of the Enlightenment, adopting instead a hermetic, anti-

humanist and pseudo-scientific language that dismissed the pursuit of meaning and purpose as bourgeois constructs.

From my studies of French literature, I must say that I never warmed to structuralism or post-structuralism, which I saw as deliberately obtuse and precious systems. Hence I agree with the views expressed above. Despite being cast aside during his own lifetime by Sartre et al., Camus still remained steadfastly true to his belief in the dignity of the human spirit. History has a way of demonstrating and proving the validity of certain stances and opinions. Camus' biographer, Olivier Todd, notes:

> Camus was opposed to 'revolutionary imperialism' and to Nazi or Fascist imperialism. Few other leftists dared to write as Camus did in 1939 that 'today the USSR can be classed among the countries that prey on others.'[2]

This was a brave pronouncement at a time when over 30 per cent of the French electorate supported the Communist party. Moral courage is a trait I associate with Camus. I have long held Camus to be a spiritual writer, a fact that is not always acknowledged by those who place him in the existentialist school, which is synonymous with atheism. Existentialism aspired to freedom and self-realisation and attempted to define morality in terms of the free, individual action rather than in terms of religion or society. The main feeling existentialist thought encourages, however, is that of absurdity, a belief that the human being alone is responsible for formulating the moral code. When one considers the prevalence of this philosophy in post-war France, riddled with guilt about the collaboration of the Vichy government with the Nazis and realising the full extent of the horror of the concentration camps, it is logical that such a world-view considered by some to be pessimistic (realistic) and dark should dominate. Camus, however, never quite buys into this black outlook. Born in Algeria, a country generously bathed in a bright and unrelenting North African sun, he was imbued with a zest for life and a desire to live the present moment to the full. Sport was his great love, especially soccer, and he enjoyed the camaraderie that vigorous physical activity engenders. It was perhaps his move to France in the lead up to the Second World War that led to Camus' feeling of being an exile, driven out of his paradise by forces that were beyond his control. He was active in the French Resistance and had obvious socialist leanings. These did not, however, blind him to the abuses that were hidden behind many ideologies. He even went so far as to claim, in his acceptance speech for the Nobel Prize for literature in 1957, that the FLN (Front de Libération Nationale) in his native Algeria had gone too far. Olivier Todd quotes this significant comment from that speech:

> I have always condemned terrorism, and I must condemn a terrorism that works blindly in the streets of Algiers and one day may strike at my mother and family. I believe in justice, but I will defend my mother before justice.[3]

Camus had a scrupulous honesty and an integrity that was lacking in Sartre. His sense of the Absolute was also very pronounced; this can be seen in many of his descriptions of nature and in the quest for authenticity that marked his journey through life. Camus realised that it was only by stripping away the unessential that one could live in a fulfilled manner. He was irreligious, if one understands by religion the sense of the divine, or the dogmas and myths that frequently surround the term. However, as Jean Onimus correctly notes:

> But there is in him the trace of a scar, even an open wound, precisely that which occurs in every lucid consciousness in the wake of 'the death of God'. The 'heart of the problem' in Camus is 'religious' if one refers by this term to what is at the origin of religions: existential anguish, the sense of guilt, the horror of death, the atrocious experience of the Absurd.[4]

This assessment goes to the core of the problem in Camus. Many of the feelings of anguish, void and despair are not confined to atheists and, in fact, characterise the spiritual itinerary of some of the great Christian mystics like Meister Eckhart and John of the Cross. Camus' quest for the truth and his struggle with the apparent meaninglessness of life after the death of God, show him to be a spiritual writer. He is read with equal profit by believers and non-believers – nowadays, these distinctions are largely redundant in any case. The increasing popularity of Camus since his death, in France and the Western world generally, can be attributed to a large extent, in my view, to the failure of organised religion to satisfy the spiritual search that many people are now engaged in and that is no longer concerned exclusively with dogmas and rituals. Value systems are breaking down everywhere; there are no longer any certainties, other than the primacy of materialistic possessions. The individual is being lost sight of in the collectivity; those who are unable or unwilling to keep up with the frenetic pace of life are left to fend for themselves. Camus doesn't shy away from the reality of the individual having to live in a merciless void but he is not prepared to deny the possibility of some degree of happiness. He even advances the thesis that Sisyphus' aimless pushing of a rock up a hill, only to see it rolling back down the slope, brings its own happiness:

> He (Sisyphus) judges that all is well. This universe where from now on he will have no master, appears to him to be neither sterile nor futile. Each of the grains that composes this rock, each mineral gleam from this mountain steeped in darkness, in themselves form a world. The struggle towards the summit is sufficient to fill a man's heart: we should imagine the possibility of Sisyphus being happy.[5]

This is sublime thinking. To illustrate Camus' sense of the Absolute, we will now turn to a brief analysis of two of his most famous works, *The Outsider* (1942) and *The Plague* (1947). Although these two novels are at first glance extremely dark and depressing, there are nonetheless signs in each of a definite search for the Absolute.

The Outsider is significant on many counts, not least being the comment made by Camus in the Preface to the novel that his hero, Meursault, a man who murders an Arab under a blinding North African sun, is the only Christ that modern society deserves. Camus obviously says this in a slightly ironical manner, because Meursault is very far removed from the figure of Christ. The criticism is directed not so much at Christ as at contemporary society which stubbornly tries to hide its nastier side and which chooses instead to live by appearances. Unlike the vast majority of men and women, Camus' hero is unable to lie. When, during his trial, he is asked if he regrets what happened on the beach where he shot the Arab, his response is totally unexpected:

> After thinking a bit, I said that what I felt was less regret than a kind of vexation – I couldn't find a better word for it.[6]

Civilised society is not used to such brutal honesty. Meursault is a kind of anti-hero, with whom the reader cannot completely identify. He remains detached from the majority of us because of his strange attitude to life, his lack of concern for social conventions, his tendency to speak his mind when silence or untruths would better serve his cause. At the beginning of the novel we see him apparently unmoved at his mother's funeral. Meursault is not even sure of exactly when she died. When he goes to the home in which she was staying, he shows no discernible sorrow. In fact, while following the funeral cortège to her last resting place, he observes: 'I caught myself thinking what an agreeable walk I might have had, if it hadn't been for Mother' (*The Outsider*, p. 21). Comments such as these are sprinkled through the book and are given added impact by the first person narration. The reader begins to sense that the protagonist is totally insensitive to the events happening around him. All he wants is for the ceremony to be concluded as quickly as possible so that he can get back to the city. The following day is a Sunday and Meursault goes for a swim, and meets Marie, with whom he had once worked and who accompanies him to a comic film that evening. They spend the night together. Much will be made of this fact at Meursault's trial. The jury will be asked how any normal person could go to a film by Fernandel the day after burying his mother. If that wasn't bad enough, Meursault then had carnal knowledge with a woman whom he scarcely knew. He is portrayed as being some sort of monster. In his Preface to the novel, Camus made this defence of his hero:

> I simply wished to state that the hero of this book is condemned because he won't play the game. In this sense he is an outsider in the eyes of the society in which he lives. He wanders about, always on the margins, because

of a private life that is both solitary and sensual, alien to the people who live at the centre.

The Meursaults of this world make others feel uncomfortable because they openly flout convention and live instinctively. They are a breed apart, exiles in a world where appearances dominate at the expense of authenticity. Meursault resembles his creator in his approach to life. He has no formal religious beliefs, but is moved when he contemplates the sea or beholds a beautiful woman. His primitive, hedonistic approach to life, his desire to be left alone to follow his instinct, run contrary to what is expected from people in civilised, sophisticated society. This is what condemns him before he ever pulls the trigger of a gun. The structure of the book is thus significant. The details of the first half of the novel are evoked again during the trial as a means of convicting Meursault of murder. His lack of emotion at his mother's funeral is presented as revealing the ruthless side of a nature that will subsequently think nothing of killing a man in cold blood. The reader knows, however, that there was nothing premeditated in this murder. Camus describes for us the fierceness of the sun beating down on Meursault, his languid movements as he wanders towards the rock behind which is situated the spring. He is like someone walking in his sleep:

> The small black lump of rock came into view far down the beach. It was rimmed by a dazzling sheen of light and feathery spray, but I was thinking of the cold, clear stream behind it, and longing to hear again the tinkle of running water. (*The Outsider*, p. 62)

Meursault did not know that he would find here the Arab with whom his friend, Raymond, had had a violent row earlier in the day. The Arab stands up and in the same movement takes out a knife which gleams in the sunlight. Meursault's head is spinning; he feels the revolver in his pocket that he had earlier taken from Raymond, and he shoots. The Arab falls to the ground and is shot four more times. We read: 'And each successive shot was another loud, fateful rap on the door of my undoing' (p. 64). 'Why', Meursault will be asked, 'did you shoot the Arab four times when he was lying defenceless on the beach?' Like Christ, Meursault is silent in the face of these accusations. In point of fact, he cannot reply to the questions he is asked, because he doesn't know exactly why he did what he did. Camus hints, at different points in the book, that if his hero had reacted differently, if he had broken down and wept, for example, when the magistrate tried to convert him by dramatically drawing his attention to the figure of the crucified Christ, if he had expressed genuine loss at the death of his mother or shown remorse for his crime, he would not have been condemned to death. But Meursault is not a communicative type of man – words condemn him as surely as silence. The magistrate cannot believe the prisoner's spiritual apathy. Even the most hardened criminals he had come across broke down when he brandished the crucifix at them. Similarly, the prison chaplain, who visits him before his execution, seeks to bring about a spiritual reconciliation in the condemned prisoner. This provokes the first obvious emotion in the hero, who ejects the priest from his cell, telling him he doesn't need the ministry of someone who isn't even a proper man. After the outburst comes some sort of catharsis, an acceptance of his fate. He thinks of his mother in a way that is far from indicating that he was indifferent to her:

> With death so near, mother must have felt like someone on the brink of freedom, ready to start life all over again.

And I, too, felt ready to start life all over again. It was as if that great rush of anger had washed me clean, emptied me of hope, and, gazing up at the dark sky spangled with its signs and stars, for the first time, the first, I laid my heart open to the benign indifference of the universe (p. 120).

The fact that Meursault makes reference to his mother at a time when he, like her, has to face the ultimate test, that of dying, shows that his relationship with her was not nearly as devoid of feeling as had been portrayed during the trial. Now that he is about to die, he remembers the things in life that gave him pleasure: the smell of Marie's hair or the pretty dresses she wore, the noises of the street, the sun setting on the sea. He knows he isn't an ogre, just a misdirected and unfortunate victim of circumstance. He does not have access to the comfort that belief in an afterlife brings to some Christians, but he does evoke the admiration of the reader for his stoicism. After all, in many ways he merely pays the price of his honesty. And he does realise a kind of liberation at the end of his journey. What lies ahead of Meursault is uncertain. We know that he hopes 'that on the day of my execution, there should be a huge crowd of spectators and that they should greet me with howls of execration' (p. 120), which is a strange desire to have before death. Meursault's hope once again casts a pessimistic and slightly odd tone on the novel. What we should remember, however, is that the person who is referred to as 'Mr Antichrist' by the magistrate is seen in a more positive light than those who sit in judgement of him. In spite of his seeming indifference to many events that happen close to him, he is more worthy of our respect than his prosecutors are. Camus reveals through his hero, or anti-hero, his ambivalent feelings towards conventional living and accepted behaviour. Often what is seen as justice is injustice: there is no clear line between good and evil. There is neither too much hope nor too much despair in *The Outsider*, just a pitiless seeking out of the truth hidden behind social and religious posturing.

The Plague contains more references to religion than *The Outsider*. The disease that grips the inhabitants of Oran is a metaphor for the *ennui* that lay at the heart of post-war France. The setting is once more North Africa and the general mood is gloomy. The third-person narrator, who is, we discover at the end of the book, Dr Rieux, the main protagonist and the person to the forefront in the struggle against the plague, notes that the first thing the plague brought to the town was exile: 'that sensation of a void within which never left us, that irrational longing to hark back to the past or else to speed up the march of time'.[7] There is an obvious sense in which the disease, which devastates the population of the town, might be construed as a punishment to the population for its sinfulness. This is the point that is frequently made by the Jesuit priest, Fr Paneloux:

> The first time this scourge appears in history, it was wielded to strike down the enemies of God. Pharaoh set himself up against the divine will, and the plague beat him to his knees. Thus from the dawn of recorded history the scourge of God has humbled the proud of heart and laid low those who hardened themselves against Him. Ponder this well, my friends, and fall on your knees. (*The Plague*, p. 80)

Increased religiosity often accompanies apocalyptic happenings, as people are faced with the unpalatable reality of their own mortality. Fr Paneloux's sermons are thus received with some trepidation by the oppressed inhabitants who listen to him. However, the eloquent priest fails to make a deep impression on Rieux. Although both are engaged in the fight to save the people from the plague, their interpretation of its origin is quite different. The doctor, a man of science, seeks out the medical causes even though he accepts that strong religious belief might aid in the fight against death. He is not frightened into becoming a believer, however; nor is he dismissive of religion *per se*. He sees that the plague helps people to rise above themselves, but this momentary heroism does little to obviate its horrific side-effects. His main problem with religion is in coming to terms with how a merciful and omnipotent God can allow the suffering and death of innocent children. Paneloux and Rieux witness one such child in the throes of death:

> Paneloux gazed down at the small mouth, fouled with the sores of the plague and pouring out the angry death-cry that has sounded through the ages of mankind. He sank to his knees, and all present found it natural to hear him say in a voice hoarse but clearly audible across that nameless, never-ending wail: 'My God, spare this child....' (p. 176)

The prayer goes unanswered and, when questioned by Rieux about the problems such a death might cause for a believer, the priest replies: 'That sort of thing is disgusting because it passes our human understanding. But perhaps we should love what we cannot understand' (p. 178). In a subsequent sermon he states that while people might be able to justify that a libertine be struck down, very few could find any reason for a child's suffering. Camus' highlighting of such fundamental spiritual issues shows him to have been a man who was embarked on a quest which involved much searching for answers to questions that were unanswerable. Loving 'what we cannot understand' is perhaps the essence of faith. Paneloux himself undergoes something of a crisis when he is struck down by the plague. We are not privy to his last thoughts but there is no doubt that he is much disillusioned by his spiritual travails. Rieux engages in many conversations of a metaphysical nature with people like Paneloux and Tarrou, the latter of whom wishes to become a saint. When it is pointed out to him that he doesn't believe in God, he states: 'Exactly. Can one be a saint without God? – that's the problem, in fact the only problem, I'm up against today' (p. 208). I have the impression that this was a dilemma that preoccupied Camus also. His strong sense of the Absolute was at variance with his experience of organised religion with its belief in a God who remains silent while children die. Rieux sees many of his friends die and is helpless to save them. When the plague finally abates, however, his assessment is far from pessimistic. He states that he decided to compile his chronicle:

> ... so that he should not be one of those who hold their peace but should bear witness in favour of those plague-stricken people; so that some memorial of the injustice and outrage done them might endure; and to state quite simply what we learn in a time of pestilence: that there are more things to admire in men than to despise. (p. 251)

This confidence in the inherent goodness of humanity distinguishes Camus from the majority of his existentialist contemporaries and gives a pronounced spiritual dimension to his writings. He sees most philosophies as being little more than religion in a different costume. He recognises that existentialism tends to glorify what crushes the human being, in that it uses reason to present an absurd and pessimistic view of existence. Camus prefers experience to reason and, while he is nowhere near as acute a philosopher as Sartre, he at least attempts to make sense of a world that has lost God and every other source of spiritual meaning. As Brian Appleyard points out:

> Camus' less spectacular wisdom was to see that, after God, it was not Mao or intellectual subtlety we needed but a simple, objective assertion of human goodness.[8]

I am not claiming any startling new insights into Camus' philosophy of life. Many readers before me have noticed the sense of the Absolute, of the sacred, in his writings. His ability to see beyond darkness to the light, his restless soul that is aware of its exile and in search of reasons to go on living, these elements mark him out as an extremely valuable spiritual witness in a period in France marked by despair. He may never have embraced the formal rituals of religious practice,[9] but his revolt against the suffering of humanity marks him out as a man of compassion and courage, a writer who almost unconsciously evokes the Absolute. He isn't impressed with grandiose words but rather with authentic witness. I conclude with the words of Rieux, who echoes the views of Camus:

> But, you know, I feel more fellowship with the defeated than with saints. Heroism and sanctity don't really appeal to me, I imagine. What interests me is – being a man. (*The Plague*, p. 209)

It's no small task being a man in a society racked with doubt and uncertainty, anguish and suffering. Rieux managed it through displaying much courage and endurance as well as a confidence in humanity that is the hallmark of his creator. Camus is ruthless in his search for the meaning of human life and courageous to the point of heroism in his expressions of the vision of the ugliness and beauty of twentieth-century living as he experienced it.

NOTES

1. *The Sunday Times,* 12 October 1997.
2. O. Todd, *Albert Camus: a Life* (trans.) Benjamin Ivry (London: Chatto & Windus, 1997), p. 90. This is a good biography of Camus, even if it tends to dwell somewhat excessively on the amorous conquests of the writer, which were legend. His life, though shortened tragically by his death in a road accident in 1960, was full and eventful.
3. Ibid., p. 378.
4. J. Onimus, *Albert Camus and Christianity* (trans.) Emmet Parker (Dublin: Gill & Macmillan, 1970), p. 4.
5. *Le Mythe de Sisyphe* (Paris: Gallimard/Idées, 1942), p. 166.
   The translation from the French is my own.
6. *The Outsider* (trans.) Stuart Gilbert (Penguin Books, 1963), p. 74. All my references will be to this edition.
7. *The Plague* (trans.) Stuart Gilbert (Penguin Books, 1960), p. 60.
8. *The Sunday Times,* 12 October 1997.
9. In the autobiographical account of his childhood and early adulthood, Camus notes how he never received any formal religious instruction at home: 'She (his mother) never spoke of God. In fact, this was a word Jacques (Camus) never heard spoken throughout his childhood, nor did he trouble himself about it. Life, so vivid and mysterious, was enough to occupy his entire being' (*The First Man* [trans.] David Hapgood, [Penguin, 1995], p. 129). What satisfied the young adolescent was insufficient for the mature man in need of more than mere life to sustain his thirst for the Absolute.

6

LOVE AND THE LOSS OF FAITH IN THE NOVELS OF KATE O'BRIEN

Kate O'Brien (1897-1974) is not to be confused with her famous, or infamous, namesake, Edna. She is a significant literary figure in the Irish context of the early years of the Free State. Her contemporaries include John McGahern, who is for me an artist of the highest calibre, and Brian Moore, whose fiction, especially *The Lonely Passion of Judith Hearne* (1955) and *I am Mary Dunne* (1968), is of an exceptionally high standard. Both McGahern and Moore, while contemporaries, were nevertheless of a different generation. O'Brien was closer in outlook and temperament to John Broderick, who was an avid admirer of her novels, as is evident from the glowing reviews he gave them in the national press. O'Brien and Broderick shared a certain traditional image of Catholic Ireland and how it impacted on middle-class families.

But Kate O'Brien has different qualities to all of the other writers mentioned above. Her decision to situate much of her fiction in the last century and in countries other than Ireland, and her feminine intuitiveness, may be contributory factors to her otherness. Like Frank McCourt, she was from Limerick, but her experiences were far removed from the city slums that he inhabited and about which he wrote. She was very much a petite bourgeoise, coming as she did from a well-to-do Catholic family. Her treatment of religion is also distinctive, as it is very difficult to detect antagonism to Catholicism in her works, although she made no secret of her agnosticism. She shares with

McGahern, Broderick and Moore the distinction of having had two of her novels banned by the Irish Censorship Board. But there the similarities end. McGahern is a marvellous chronicler of rural Ireland in the fifties and sixties. His characters possess qualities that transcend time and place, have a universality that make them live in our memories. They are as though moulded by their rough physical environment. John Broderick evokes the scheming and prosperous provincial middle class which emerged in rural Ireland after Independence. He is antagonistic to the money-grabbing, sanctimonious and censorious attitudes that characterised this social grouping. For him, the Catholic clergy was but an extension of the bourgeoisie. Brian Moore is very skilled at evoking the sectarian divide in the Belfast of his youth. That said, Moore is more concerned with individual dilemmas than he is with societal tensions.

So what is special about Kate O'Brien? She was born some years before the other novelists to whom we have referred, in 1897. Her father was a wealthy horse-dealer and her mother died when she was only five. This necessitated her being sent at a very young age to be educated by the nuns at Laurel Hill Convent, in Limerick. The period she spent under the nuns' care influenced her literary formation. She admitted that she enjoyed the experience. In one of her best novels, *The Land of Spices* (1941), she describes how an English Reverend Mother, Helen Archer, takes a special interest in the youngest inmate of her school, Anna Murphy, whose sad life in some ways mirrors her own. Anna's parents are no longer a loving couple and the young girl senses this. She thus turns to the Reverend Mother when she has to endure the trauma of the death of her favourite brother in a freak swimming accident. A strong bond develops between the two. Thus, the nun insists that Anna take up the University Scholarship she has won, in spite of the opposition of her grandmother, who doesn't see the value of further education for young ladies and who wants to place her niece in a bank. Mère Marie-Hélène issues this warning:

> Our Order is world-wide and powerful, Mrs Condon, and it takes care of its children. That is its *raison d'être*. And Anna is very particularly our child. We shall look after her, and she can rest assured that between us and the Bishop, means will be found to prevent her becoming a clerk in the Four Provinces Bank.[1]

In addition to being a forceful character, this nun is also politically astute and realises that, by enlisting the support of the bishop, she will bring Mrs Condon, who has a brother a priest anxious for ecclesiastical advancement, to heel. She thus ensures the academic development of one of her students. *The Land of Spices* is a very sensitive and readable account of convent life from both the students' and the nuns' point of view. It is easy to forget the huge contribution the female religious orders made to educating generations of young Irish women. Kate O'Brien had an obvious liking for, and understanding of, nuns, unlike Edna O'Brien, whose experience at their hands was very negative. Is it not slightly paradoxical that a novelist like Kate O'Brien, whom many commentators like to portray as some kind of lesbian/feminist icon, is very sympathetic in her treatment of nuns and priests? She doesn't blame the way she was taught religion for her subsequent loss of faith. The scandal provoked by the scene where the young Helen Archer returns home early from school one day to find her father and his acolyte, Etienne, 'in the embrace of love' (p. 157), seems very tame indeed by today's standards. And yet this one line ensured the banning of the book in Ireland and the frenzied attack on its author in the Senate by a certain Professor McGuinness. Kate O'Brien did not set out to shock sensibilities or to debunk myths. She preferred to depict moral dilemmas as she saw them, revolving normally around the choice between following one's instinct and facing up to one's social or religious duties. In this chapter I deal principally with the treatment of love and religion in Kate O'Brien's fiction. These two elements reflect, I believe, the nostalgia the author felt for her lost faith. When you have been imbued with Catholic dogmas throughout your youth and early adulthood, it is difficult to eradicate them fully from your mind. The influence lingers, the old reflexes remain, even when faith has disappeared. Kate O'Brien was cognisant of the integral role of the Catholic religion in the lives of the vast majority of the Irish men and women of her time. Not all aspects of the institutional Church appealed to her. She saw the insular dogmatic attitude of many of the clergy, some of which is incapsulated in the pronouncements of Fr Conroy, the chaplain to the Compagnie de la Sainte Famille, a Belgian order, who states to Reverend Mother:

> Irish national life is bound up with its religion, and it may well be that educational work will become difficult here soon for those Orders who adhere too closely to a foreign tradition. (*The Land of Spices*, p. 15)

The young priest, fresh out of the Maynooth seminary, irritates Mère Marie-Hélène, who makes no apology for her efforts to promote *La Politesse* in her girls, that is to say, the ability to mix comfortably in international as well as national circles, to have well-informed opinions and good social skills. She steers them clear of insular and parochial prejudice where at all possible. Her personal conflicts are hidden from the students but shared with the reader: her tendency to be too severe in her judgements of others and her constant wrestling with the vow of obedience. The greatest obstacle she encounters in her spiritual life is that posed by human love:

And, free in her meditations on God's will, and His hopes for humanity, she admitted that human love – such love, for instance, as she would have protested she felt for her father when she was young – must almost always offend the heavenly lover by its fatuous egotism. (*The Land of Spices*, p. 20)

Her treatment of human love provides a very clear insight into Kate O'Brien's world-view. Human love is imperfect for her because it is wrapped up in egotism and tainted with sin. It compares very unfavourably with the love of God, which is eternal. Very seldom do we come across a portrayal of love between a man and a woman that is in any way a microcosm of divine love in O'Brien's novels. We will now see how this area is dealt with in a subtly different way in two well-known novels, *The Ante-Room* (1934) and *Mary Lavelle* (1936), the latter of which was banned by the Irish Censorship Board.

The Ante-Room is Kate O'Brien's second novel and follows the highly successful *Without My Cloak*, a sort of Irish version of *The Forsythe Saga*, and which won both the Hawthornden Prize and the James Tait Memorial Prize. The fortunes of the Considines, a rich merchant family from Mellick (the name O'Brien gives Limerick), form the basis of the first novel. In *The Ante-Room*, Teresa Considine, married to Danny Mulqueen, is dying of an incurable cancer. Her suffering is all the more acute for the realisation that she will be abondoning her son, Reggie, savaged by syphilis, to a cruel and uncaring world:

Reggie was 36, wasted, unhappy, dangerous – dependent for his own decency and for his whole interest in life, on his devotion to her – and she was leaving him – and God had not answered her yet or told her where he was to turn then, so that he would do no harm in his weakness, and yet might be a little happy, a little less than desolate.[2]

The novel traces the many conflicts that arise as the characters struggle with the twists and turns that life throws at them. Teresa's major concern is a very unselfish and natural one: to ensure that her son is cared for after her death. The importance of property, family relationships and responsibilities, the fine psychological probing of the motivations that prompt people to act in a certain manner, remind one of François Mauriac, who revelled in depicting the labyrinth that is family in novels like *Thésèse Desqueyroux* and *Le Noeud de Vipères*. Like Mauriac, O'Brien is also adept at analysing the problems that inclinations of the flesh bring to bear on her protagonists. The main character of *The Ante-Room*, Agnes Mulqueen, is in love with her sister's husband, Vincent de Courcy O'Regan. The latter becomes irritated at his wife's tendency to flee to Roseholm, the Mulqueens' residence, every time they have a serious quarrel. Marie-Rose, thanks to Agnes' love and attention, is then able to return, 'her petals dewy and refreshed, to subjugate again the perverse and irritable stranger who was her husband' (p. 30). Vincent begins to ache for similar comfort, and from the same source. At the beginning of the novel, we discover that Agnes is desperately trying to exorcise the love she feels for Vincent, which she knows to be wrong. John Cronin provides a perceptive assessment of her predicament:

> Agnes has to choose between her guilty desire for Vincent, her loyalty to her faith and her long-standing love for her sister.[3]

Her situation is made even more difficult when her mother's brother, Canon Considine, announces that he is to say a Triduum of Masses at Roseholm. Agnes knows that the thoughts she has been harbouring for her brother-in-law are sinful and will thus prevent her from receiving Communion, unless she goes to Confession. She owes it to her mother to participate fully in the Triduum. She also knows that Vincent will be accompanying Marie-Rose to Roseholm and that she will need all the sanctifying power of grace to be able to deal with his presence. After Benediction, she waits in the church to cleanse herself of her sin: 'Be clean and free of it, and filled with prayer, before she see his dreaded face again' (*The Ante-Room*, p. 51). This is what she hopes to achieve through the sacrament. The priest, a Jesuit, on hearing her admission of illicit lust, explains how human love is finite 'whereas in the idea of God there is matter for eternity'. Agnes receives momentary respite from this thought but will remark ruefully to herself later:

> Yes, holy Jesuit, that's all very fine. But we aren't made in the most convenient form in which to pursue ideas, and we have no notion at all of how to front eternity.
> (*The Ante-Room*, p. 200)

Spirit and flesh, human life and eternity, good and evil, all these opposites are in plentiful supply throughout the novel. We have Teresa dying upstairs with her family gathered round her, the canon saying his Masses in the house, Dr Curran and Vincent vying for Agnes' love, Marie-Rose suffering abandonment by her husband, Reggie's increasing infatuation with his mother's nurse, Miss Cunningham, the palpable religiosity of the household – there is much indeed to hold the reader's attention in this complex plot. There is much to appreciate also in O'Brien's capacity to present what is unique in all her characters; their hopes and fears, strengths and weaknesses. Religion is omnipresent as a kind of sub-plot or motif. O'Brien knows the power of the sacrifice of the Mass on believers. Canon Considine has an enraptured audience:

> Silence relaxed into quietude. God was present; the room and the morning were full of peace. The Latin murmuring of the priest, the holy sighs of old Bessie, the prayerful sibilations of Sister Emmanuel, softly relaxing tension, brought back its human reality to each consciousness, though keeping it mercifully illumined by the miracle in which it was participant. (*The Ante-Room*, p. 175)

This is powerful writing, bringing into focus how love in its earthly form can never bring this quality of peace. Nurse Cunningham's calculated decision to accept Reggie's marriage proposal, 'warts and all', is perceived as sordid by Agnes, but at least it is honest and hurts nobody. In fact, it brings peace to Teresa, who 'was purely happy, entirely and childishly grateful to God, …because her ruined son would have a custodian when she was gone' (p. 288). For Vincent and Agnes there can be no such happy resolution; only a flaming passion that can neither be consummated nor quenched. Agnes' senses are disturbed by the touch of Vincent's hand and she knows that she could realise her most exotic dreams with him as her partner, but at what price?

> She stood up and paced her room. Here were Christian and social duty combining with sisterly love to make one foolish craving of hers impossible. And she with brains and blood and training found them justified and her desire insane. It followed it must die – but how quickly? (*The Ante-Room*, p. 240)

A possible alternative to Vincent is Dr Curran, but Agnes doesn't love him, cannot bring herself to love him. Vincent provides an unexpected solution by commiting suicide in such a way as to make it appear an accident. However, Agnes knows that Vincent's death was no accident and her suffering is even more intense for the knowledge that she is responsible for it. She had admitted to Curran shortly before Vincent's suicide: 'I feel as if I had some kind of poison – as if I were dying here this minute – half dead' (p. 299). Now her desolation is even greater. In fact, it is not love itself that is of the greatest importance for Agnes, but the sense of sin attendant on such love and the way it gnaws on her conscience. There is no liberation here, only pain and suffering.

Whereas Agnes stops short of following her natural inclinations and desires, Mary Lavelle steps outside of conventional rules and restrictions in search of the *grand amour*. The daughter of a widowed doctor, who is petty, self-pitying and tyrannical, the heroine escapes the stifling ambience of provincial Ireland and a fiancé whom she doesn't really love, to spend a year as a Miss to a noble Spanish family. Her journey becomes an initiation to a new culture, with its naked violence exemplified by the ritual of the bullfight ring, as well as the flowering of a sensuousness that had been kept well under wraps in Catholic Ireland. It is clear from Mary's motivation for going abroad that she fears being tied to a restrictive mode of existence:

> To cease being a daughter without immediately becoming a wife. To be a free lance, to belong to no one place or family or person – to achieve that silly longing of childhood, only for one year, before she flung it with all the other childish things upon the scrapheap.[4]

Had Agnes Mulqueen realised her ambition to travel, who knows what her fate might have been. She may well have experienced the liberation and exhilaration that come to Mary Lavelle. They are both faced with a similar moral choice. In Mary's case, the object of her desire is not her sister's husband, but rather the happily married son of the family for which she is acting as Miss. Her loyalty to John, her fiancé, rapidly evaporates as she falls madly in love with Juanito, an idealistic, moral young man, destined to be 'one of Spain's great men'. Possessing as he does lofty principles and a strong sense of honour, this is not the sort of man to give in easily to a passing fancy. Mary Lavelle's arrival in Spain will not only disturb the equilibrium of Juanito, but also that of his father, Don Pablo, who sees in the young Irishwoman the 'eternal poetic myth of girlhood' and who is immediately smitten with her.

Mary Lavelle is not as finely sculpted a novel as *The Ante-Room*. Too many incidents in the narrative stretch the credulity of the reader. We are expected to believe that a shy, largely inexperienced and uncultivated young woman has the power to woo what are essentially two highly sophisticated men. I am not claiming that love at first sight is a myth, but I do have reservations about the instantaneous attraction that is ignited in the look that Mary and Juanito exchange as she climbs the stairs to her room on the first night she meets him:

> These two were to know each other hereafter, and to arrive at their knowledge in reluctance, grief and protestation. Long pain lay ahead of the unwitting sympathy with which the eyes of each unprompted sought the aspect of the other, but for this once, if never again, they were innocent. (*Mary Lavelle*, p.145)

O'Brien does not usually give such licence to her omniscient narrator. Most of the plot is revealed to us in the lines above. Juanito falls in love with Mary, seeks out ways to meet her alone, whisks her off in his car on a day she is meant to be visiting Toledo. Instead, they spend the time luxuriating in each other's company, in the strength of their shared passion. They acknowledge that there is no future for their love, and yet they keep on imagining how happy they might have been in different circumstances. Mary says to her lover:

> If you were an American, say, and your wife had a little lost
> her interest in you, and divorce was part of the code and
> religion you were brought up in, and would not displace
> your ambitions and ideals, and make you into a kind of
> exile without occupation – then you and I might have a
> kind of clumsy future to discuss. (*Mary Lavelle*, p. 254)

The emphasis has shifted sharply from that seen in *The Ante-Room*. Mary would be quite prepared to sin against Catholic teaching and enter into a sexual relationship with Juanito. What holds her back is the danger that in so doing she could 'for ever maim a handsome and self-confident man of twenty-nine' (p. 257). She has no fear whatever in relation to herself, but cannot bear the thought of injuring the peace of mind and self-respect of Juanito. Religious constraints do not enter in a serious manner into Mary's moral framework, unlike in the case of Agnes Mulqueen. In fact, she does eventually have sex with Juanito, on the eve of her proposed departure date for Ireland, and she does not suffer remorse afterwards.

> She lay under his hands and marvelled at her peace. She
> thought of school and home, of John, of God's law and
> sin, and did not let herself discard such thoughts. They
> existed, as real and true as ever, with all their conditional
> claims on her – but this claim was his, and she would
> answer it taking the consequences (*Mary Lavelle*, p. 308).

In her liberated stance, she resembles the novelist, who is quite daring in her description of the love-making, which takes up several pages, even though everything is couched in very tasteful and poetic language. It is easy to imagine how, in 1936, Mary Lavelle's 'fall from grace' may have provoked something of a scandal. More shocking again, however, was the confession of her lesbian love by another Miss, Agatha Conlon, to the heroine:

> Are you shocked? I like you the way a man would, you see. I never see you without wanting to touch you…. It's a sin to feel like that.

To which Mary replies:

> Oh, everything's a sin! (*Mary Lavelle*, p. 285)

This type of exchange explains to some extent what makes *Mary Lavelle* an exciting departure in terms of dealing with taboo subjects like lesbianism – without the slightest hint of condemnation on the part of the novelist. What Conlon feels for Mary is seen as no better or worse than what passes between Mary and Juanito, or Agnes and Vincent: 'Everything is a sin', after all. Love is mainly a source of unhappiness for Kate O'Brien's characters, many of whom break free of their Catholic upbringing to do things that could imperil their eternal salvation. Is what they do wrong? The novelist does not choose to pronounce on such matters. The raising of these issues was a bold step at a time when a Jansenistic distrust of the flesh was prevalent in Ireland and when the Censorship Board was particularly active. So where did this leave Kate O'Brien in relation to the Catholic Church? In his excellent analysis of Irish culture in the years 1930-60, Brian Fallon notes his belief that Kate O'Brien seems to have kept her religious faith, which had been mellowed by her experience of continental Catholicism, and adds:

> Her novels remain especially valuable because they depict the impact of the Church on thinking, educated middle class women, through the medium of nuns as well as the

male clergy. She spoke to and for people who, while they might be critical of many of the Church's sayings and doings, still counted themselves believing Catholics in spiritual communion with millions around the world.[5]

Mr Fallon rightly mentions this group of thinking Irish Catholics who saw themselves as belonging to a wider church and who weren't afraid to take a critical stance when they weren't in agreement with certain dictates. He is also correct in pointing to the positive influence of the nuns and male clergy on Irish women like Kate O'Brien. He rightly points to her experience of living abroad as having shaped a different, more continental form of Catholicism in her. Her feminist leanings can be seen in the value she attached to education for women as well as their right to independence and self-determination. Characters like Mary Lavelle choose their own destiny and accept the consequences of their actions. They are no blushing virgins, no innocents in the ways of the world, that is to say, once they are initiated into such rituals. Yet, for all their independence there lurks within them a close identification with the Catholic religion, albeit in a sanitised form. In *Pray for the Wanderer* (1938), written partly as a response to the banning of *Mary Lavelle*, we meet Nell, a devout Catholic, whose virginity is dependent less on piety than on the conviction that the Church's teaching is appropriate in many ethical situations. Without the moral framework provided by organised religion, she feels, the slip towards an unswerving liberalism is a great danger:

> Adultery and homosexuality were entirely respectable so long as their practitioners had the *savoir-faire* to keep them so. Any joke whatever was acceptable, so long as it was a good joke. Any word permissible almost anywhere, by either sex. But tolerance and discretion

were the passwords in regard to actual life. Go as you please and make no scenes.[6]

These views have more than a little relevance in contemporary Ireland where political correctness is *de rigueur*. Nobody anymore wants to criticise or denounce, and to declare that some action is sinful will only be greeted with scorn. That type of vocabulary has all but disappeared in this country. Kate O'Brien saw a liberal strain developing in the Irish Catholic merchant class to which she belonged in the 1930s. Her self-imposed exile clearly assisted her in making an objective appraisal of the country she had left. Her writings transport the reader to a universe that is both foreign and familiar. Her characters encounter the sort of difficulties that still beset us today: the universal, inevitable struggle between the spirit and the flesh, the quest to find a spiritual meaning in a world that is hostile to spirituality, preoccupied as it is with materialistic advancement at all costs. Matt, the writer-hero of *Pray for the Wanderer*, lives in London but returns home to Ireland when his relationship with a married actress concludes (another failed couple in Kate O'Brien). He hopes he might find some certainty in the country of his birth. Matt has problems. He is attracted to Nell, his brother's sister-in-law, but narrowly fails in his attempts to woo her. The main obstacle he encouters is Nell's stubborn attachment to Catholicism.

> He on the other hand 'believed in impulse, pursuit and danger; high fences and blind riding; the courage to race life as it flies. It was because of all these faiths that his greatest faith was in personal liberty – a faith that had finally driven him out of the Church, but made it impossible for him to find any resting place in conremporary life (pp. 218-9).

He is in many ways the mouthpiece of O'Brien because of his ambivalent attitude to Ireland:

> Could he live in de Valera's Ireland, where the artistic conscience is ignored – merely because, artist or not, he loved that Ireland, its lovely face, its trailing voice, its ribaldry and piety and dignified sense of wide spaciousness of time? (*Pray for the Wanderer*, p. 248)

Matt's answer to this rhetorical question, like that of the novelist who gave him life, was an emphatic, if nostalgic, 'No'. We can see that faith and personal liberty do not marry in Kate O'Brien's fiction. Far too often characters discover their paths blocked by some religious obstacles. Whenever love is properly tasted and enjoyed it is usually in some foreign setting. Ireland, for all its attractions, is a cultural backwater and a puritanical state. Independence had not improved the lot of Irish people in Kate O'Brien's optic. Thus it was that she died in England in 1974, largely impoverished and in poor health. I am glad to have met her through her novels, as she has keen insights into many basic human issues and writes with a classical style. I was delighted to discover recently that *The Land of Spices* is to feature on the Leaving Certificate English syllabus because it will reveal to students a hidden Ireland that doesn't appear in most of the Irish fiction of this century. She probably has more in common with the realist tradition of the nineteenth century than she does with any twentieth century movement. At times she reminds one of Flaubert. Perhaps Emma Bovary's futile quest for love was an influence on O'Brien's approach to loss. Because, although Flaubert's character embarks on adulterous affairs and hurts her husband and daughter, she is portrayed as a woman who is frustrated in her attempts to find the romantic love of her dreams. Even the most skeptical reader has to feel some sympathy with her plight. Her mystical cravings meet with as little success as her amorous exploits. Irish society, like the provincial world of Emma Bovary, presented many obstacles to the realisation of romantic fantasies, as Matt points out to Nell:

> Listen. If you marry me, you'd be doing an extraordinary thing. You believe in all the mysteries of the Catholic Church and in its absolute moral authority. You also believe in a whole tissue of minor taboos and obligations and prohibitions which derive from your central belief, and also from being a citizen of Dev's Free State and a victim of the universal *Zeitgeist* (*Pray for the Wanderer*, p. 240).

This is not a particularly positive presentation of Irish society at the beginning of the Free State. Everything revolves around taboos with regard to sexuality and sin, largely as a result of a dominant and inward-looking attitude on the part of the Church and political leaders. Love and faith are placed in opposition to each other; they are presented as being somehow incompatible. It is significant that as a novelist Kate O'Brien refrains from allowing her own loss of faith (or at least her serious doubting of many aspects of it) to appear in any obvious manner in what she writes. Reviewing Lorna Reynolds' literary portrait of Kate O'Brien, John Broderick offered this astute assessment of her place and prominence in Irish letters:

> For over a century the Catholic middle class have been the dominant influence in Ireland; and for the past 65 years, the ruling class also. Yet, they have been little written about; and compared with the bourgeoisie in France and England, who have produced, with a few exceptions, all the great novelists of the last two centuries, they have been singularly slow in producing creative

writers. It is true that they have given birth to the greatest novelist of the century in Joyce; but he is outside the mainstream of fiction; and of writers to compare with novelists like Mrs Gaskill, Trollope, Galsworthy, Graham Greene and Evelyn Waugh, there have been but few. Of these Kate O'Brien is the best known; and also, I think, the best.[7]

NOTES

1. *The Land of Spices* (London: Virago, 1988), p. 262.
2. *The Ante-Room* (London: Virago, 1989), p. 17.
3. John Cronin, *The Anglo-Irish Novel*, vol. 2, 1900-1940 (Belfast: Appletree Press, 1990), p. 145.
4. *Mary Lavelle* (London: Virago, 1984), p. 34.
5. *An Age of Innocence. Irish Culture 1930-1960* (Dublin: Gill and Macmillan, 1998), p. 192.
6. *Pray for the Wanderer* (Bath: Cedric Chivers, 1969), pp. 108-9.
7. *Irish Independent*, 17-18 April 1987.

7

JOHN BRODERICK: IRISH NOVELIST IN THE EUROPEAN TRADITION

Many readers will know very little about the Athlone novelist, John Broderick (1924-89), and yet he is the author of some thirteen novels, several critical and travel articles in *The Irish Times* and someone who deserves more critical recognition than he has attracted to date. His first novel, *The Pilgrimage* (1961), elicited the type of praise that Julien Green, the French-born writer of American extraction, normally only lavished on deceased classical writers. Green and Broderick were friends – the former speaks glowingly of a visit to Athlone in the 1950s in his *Journal* – but this fact alone does not explain the genuine enthusiasm Broderick's first novel aroused in him. In the Preface to the French translation of *The Pilgrimage*, Green notes:

> It is an extraordinarily captivating book. I acknowledge, however, that it might have the capacity to shock certain readers. In it we see religion and vice interwoven, even though the narrator always maintains an extremely serious tone. We meet an inadequate clergy and lay people whose sole preoccupation is to avoid Hell…. If I were a critic, I would write about this book.[1]

As I said, such praise was unusual from the first foreigner to be elected to the Académie Française and one of the leading figures in French twentieth-century letters. Green's silence about any of Broderick's subsequent works probably demonstrates a declension in the standard of the latter's writings after this promising start. Green's enthusiasm, however, was not shared by the Irish Literary Censorship Board, which saw fit to ban *The Pilgrimage* because it contained 'material with the potential to corrupt'. It is difficult now to see anything unduly offensive to public morality in *The Pilgrimage*, almost four decades later. Irish society has evolved greatly in the intervening period. The Catholic Church is no longer as powerful a force; our entry into Europe and improved communications have broadened our views on morality and there is no longer the same close identification of nationalism and Catholicism. Contraception has been legalised, as has divorce, and homosexuality decriminalised. One is left to wonder how Broderick would have fared in this new ambience.

His homosexuality has been fairly well documented, but it would be wrong to think that his sexual preferences placed him in the avant-garde category. Broderick was fiercely conservative in religious matters and especially in the reverence he displayed towards the Eucharist. He disliked the changes wrought by Vatican II and, as Patrick Murray points out, he often began his diatribes on the developments in the Catholic Church with the comment: 'Before the Mass was abolished!'[2] It is clear then that there were many paradoxes and much pain in the life of this man. Like his friend, Julien Green, his sexuality and his spirituality were placed in opposition to one another in a classical confrontation of the spirit and the flesh. His devotion to his mother bordered on reverence and he must have suffered greatly at the premature death of his father (when he was only three) and the remarriage of Mrs Broderick to the manager of the family bakery ten years later. The Freudian interpretations of the effects of this perceived abandonment by his mother are too obvious to dwell on in any detail in this chapter. It is sufficient to note that Broderick carried with him throughout his life a tortured aspect that betrayed his inner turmoil.

This explains to some extent the vehemence with which he set about attacking hypocrisy in all its guises. In a television interview on RTÉ with Patrick Gallagher, shortly before he moved to Bath in the eighties, Broderick admitted: 'I've been a hypocrite for years.' He explained this by saying that he went to Mass on Sundays mainly in order to please his mother and because he knew that if he didn't go, it could adversely affect the family business. He was hurt by the banning of *The Pilgrimage*, which was a well-constructed and promising first novel. The only slightly *risqué* elements in this book were the subtle hints with regard to the homosexuality of some of the characters and the extramarital affairs in which the main female protagonist, Julia Glynn, engages. These two elements were enough to involve the censor. Julia Glynn is married to a man several years her senior, who is crippled with arthritis. During their honeymoon Julia has reason to suspect her husband's homosexuality by the intense relationship he engages in with a German. (She finds correspondence from the latter when tidying away some of her husband's things years later.) Happy with the freedom that being married to a rich builder affords her, Julia, as soon as her husband becomes incapacitated, renews her sexual relationship with her husband's nephew, Jim, a doctor, who comes once a week to tend to his uncle. The departure of Stephen, the manservant who is secretly in love with Julia, to drive Fr Victor, another weekly visitor to the invalid, to the local monastery is the signal for Julia and Jim to make love hurriedly and in a manner that is almost impersonal.

Her comfortable existence gets upset when she begins receiving anonymous letters which describe in lurid detail her relationship with Jim. The novel takes on the heightened drama and tension of a detective yarn as we begin to wonder who is responsible for these letters. In the end, Julia discovers that it is Stephen, almost mad with jealousy, who is her tormentor. At this stage she has already entered into a sexual relationship with the manservant. Julia is aware of Stephen's incapacity to have any type of normal healthy sexual relationship with her:

> She doubted if Stephen, who, she had no doubt, loved her in his own fashion, would ever be able to dissociate lovemaking from the furtive, the sordid and the unclean. The puritanism which was bred in their bones, and encouraged in their youth by every possible outside pleasure, was never entirely eradicated.[3]

Broderick admitted that François Mauriac was the only literary influence of which he was aware,[4] and certainly there are similarities in the way the two depict the hypocritical materialistic characteristics of the middle class to which they both belonged. There is also a Jansenistic distrust of the flesh evident in their novels. The quote above is very insightful into a certain race of Irishmen who had a strongly puritanical streak, seeing sex as sordid and sinful. This is an attitude that is not nearly as prevalent among the young Irish people of today, who have probably gone as far in the other direction, in that they see very little connection between sexual concourse and sin. In fact, the whole idea of sin has become very blurred in Ireland and it is rare indeed that you hear priests or lay people making explicit reference to it. In contrast, the majority of people living in the Ireland of the 1960s knew about, and had a genuine fear of, sin and eternal damnation. In this context I think it is appropriate to refer to the experiences of an Irish Redemptorist priest, Fr Tony Flannery, who noted in a recent publication that people of his generation were encouraged to see the body as bad, the source of all the troublesome passions:

> We were taught to think badly of ourselves. Instead of focusing on the goodness of God, which is where all Christian teaching should begin, we were first told of our own sinfulness. And the emphasis on sexual sin... led us to be ill at ease with our own bodies.[5]

Broderick frequently evokes the strong reservations and residue of guilt of his characters with regard to sex. They find it well nigh impossible to reconcile the two. The problem, from a literary standpoint, however, is that Broderick makes his feelings too apparent to his readers and so ruins all pretence of objectivity. In general, he fails to disguise adequately his hurt and alienation. Too often he feels compelled to spell things out for his reader. As Michael Paul Gallagher, one of the few critics to write on Broderick, points out:

> The tendency to become not simply an unJamesian intrusive narrator but a downright domineering narrator is a major pitfall in Broderick's approach to fiction.[6]

This approach can be explained to a certain extent by Broderick's painful experience of Irish provincial life and of the narrow-minded and vindictive nature of its inhabitants. Many Irish writers before him had chosen exile as a means of escaping from a cultural milieu that attempted to stifle all artistic endeavour and creativity – Joyce is the main figure that comes to mind in this respect. He chose exile as a means of nourishing his art and he revelled in writing about Ireland from his self-imposed banishment. Many others followed his example. More than in any other country, perhaps, the writer in Ireland was suspect, especially when living in a Church-dominated society which liked to do its thinking for the people and which didn't tolerate opposition to its authority. The tension became all the more intolerable when the artist chose to delve into aspects of the human condition that were seen to be the domain of the Church – particularly the whole area of sexuality. In Broderick's case, the suspicion of his writings was magnified by his homosexuality, a subject that he dealt with openly in his fiction but that he declined to dwell on publicly in real life. Like his friend Julien Green, he was a very spiritual man who found it impossible to reconcile his religious convictions with the urgings of the flesh. He remarked once in an interview:

> I think the Irish are pathological about homosexuality. That was one of the reasons why I chose it as the theme for my books because it had never been done before.[7]

Having been born into a wealthy Athlone family who owned the local bakery, Broderick was afforded the luxury of travelling abroad, where he encountered a far more enlightened attitude to sex and religion. He particularly liked the freedom of Paris, where he made the acquaintance of such literary luminaries as Samuel Beckett, Gore Vidal, Ernest Hemingway, as well as Mauriac and Green. Paris attracted artists from all over the world and Broderick marvelled at how different this cosmopolitan world was from Brinsley MacNamara's *Valley of the Squinting Windows* (1918), which captured in a succinct manner rural Ireland at the turn of the century. Broderick greatly resented that Irish society he associated with: 'the isolationism and xenophobia of Irish nationalism, the puritanism and authoritarianism of the Irish Catholic Church and the striving for respectability of the Irish middle classes.'[8] There you have it – Irish nationalism, a controlling Church and emerging middle class all combining to stifle creative thinking.

As well as the Catholic Church, Broderick resented the insular attitudes that prevailed in parts of the midlands, and in rural Ireland in general. In *The Fugitives* (1962), the heroine returns to Ireland after spending many years abroad and is immediately struck by the oppressive ambience of the place:

> She found it hard to remember what it was like to live in this town. The certainty, the nullity, the watchfulness, the serpentine relationships of people who knew each other too well: the ultimate choice between hypocrisy and complete acceptance of the written and unwritten code.[9]

This is a fine description of the enclosed and watchful atmosphere of many Irish provincial towns in the middle of the twentieth century. Being from this background himself, Broderick was writing about the familiar, and this is what makes some of his satire all the more biting. His themes are constant: the Jansenistic attitude to sexuality among Irish people, the snobbery of the new middle class and their manic desire to climb the social ladder, the dominance of the Catholic Church in matters ranging from politics to agriculture, from economics to sexual morality. When he tackles these themes, his anger and bitterness show through. His caricature of the middle classes is too often transparent and didactic and the excessive intervention of the omniscient and inartistic narrator serves to damage the moral integrity of his texts – Mauriac would never fall into that particular trap. In *Don Juaneen*, we witness Broderick's tone when he describes the wealthy O'Connor couple:

> Their whole life was permeated with a profound and largely unconscious hypocrisy. Money was the only God they worshipped; *although, pious and bigoted Catholics as they were, they would have been horrified if anyone had told them so.*[10]

The last few comments betray a negativity not only to the characters he is describing but also to the literary process itself. It's as if he cannot trust his readers to make a correct evaluation of what is presented to them. This is undoubtedly the main weakness in Broderick as a novelist. On the plus side, however, there is his ability to tackle problems associated with sexuality. We have seen how Julia Glynn is largely devoid of guilt when it comes to sex outside marriage. In her liberated attitude, she ressembles closely Marie Fogarty, the heroine of what is undoubtedly Broderick's best-known (if not his most accomplished) novel, *An Apology for Roses* (1973). Marie enters into an affair with the local curate, Fr Tom Moran, whom she continues to use (or abuse), in spite of his sexual ineptitude: 'because his large well-endowed body excited her; a body perfectly fashioned for the intimacies which stirred her imagination, filling her senses with a primitive phallic longing.'[11]

It was not at all commonplace, even at the beginning of the 1970s revolution, to speak in such forthright terms about sexuality, and to refer to affairs with priests (whose sexual prowess is clearly outlined) was especially daring. Many of Broderick's female characters have an insatiable sexual appetite. I believe that Julien Green's portrayal of Moïra, his most famous character, who, we are told, 'is what the Romans called lupa, a beast perpetually famished',[12] influenced Broderick in his portrayal of women. Broderick freely admitted his predilection for this particular novel by Green. Broderick is very explicit in some of his descriptions of sex and he depicts many women who seek their sexual pleasure from any sort of male, as long as his body is suitable. As a homosexual, female sexuality may have been foreign to his experience. (That said, I know several homosexual male writers who write very well about female sexuality.) And yet this does not prevent him from coming up with some almost comical scenes that are hard to resist. In *The*

Pride of Summer (1976), we encounter the insatiable and pious Kitty O'Reilly, whose lowly-sexed husband, Frank, is forced to satisfy his wife's longings:

> This litany went on as Frank allowed his clothes to be clawed off him by the eager, predatory fingers of his 'lonely' little wife, who fell back upon the bed murmuring a prayer to the Holy Ghost as her husband thrust himself into her quivering body with an ardour she had not experienced for years.... Twice she writed in 'agony', the word she always used when in the throes of an orgasm.[13]

This account, though amusing, borders on the pornographic. Note the vocabulary used to build up the impression of the beast-like woman: she has 'claws' and fingers that are 'eager' and 'predatory'. While such descriptions could be considered comical caricatures, they do betray nonetheless an ambivalent attitude to women and to sexuality in general. Many of Broderick's female characters seek solace in a type of brutal sex, but their unbridled promiscuity leads them to the conclusion that the only ultimate fate that awaits them is aloneness. They are alone even when they are having sex because it is sexual activity devoid of love. Love and sex do not intermingle in Broderick's novels.

There are other extremes of women portrayed by Broderick also. For example, Agnes Fogarty, Marie's mother, shrinks at the thought of sexual contact with her husband. She is at the other end of the sexual spectrum from her daughter:

> She closed her eyes again, shutting out the Sacred Heart, as her memory recalled the first terrible years of marriage when, a frigid woman, she had discovered with horror

the insatiable appetite of her husband. He was little better than an animal, worse in fact since animals did not have souls, and could not be held responsible for their filth.[14]

Note the way that, for Agnes, sex and religion are set in opposition to one another. When forced even to contemplate the sex act, she has to shut out the image of the Sacred Heart. Intercourse is reduced to an animalistic ritual to which she is forced to submit but from which she remains detached. As is true of Mauriac and Julien Green, there are very few, if any, happy couples in Broderick's novels, and even less love. What love does exist occurs between male couples, and these are subjected to the censorious and intolerant attitude of the so-called 'normal' people who see fit to sit in judgement of them. Homosexual love is of the unnatural, unmentionable kind for heterosexuals, who are involved in many cases in far more depraved relationships. In *The Trial of Father Dillingham* (1982), Maurice and Eddie look on their love for one another as: 'a recompense which they owed to one another as outcasts and aliens in a hostile world.'[15] *The Waking of Willie Ryan* (1965) sees the main character committed to a mental asylum by his family, with the connivance of the local priest, Fr Mannix, because he has been engaged in a homosexual relationship with a widower. He returns home from the mental hospital after twenty-five years with the intention of gaining revenge. His family, in this once more similar to many bourgeois families depicted by Mauriac, is concerned more with appearances than with truth. Marginals like Willie, with their tendency to fly in the face of order, disturb social equilibrium and make his family uncomfortable. But the complicity of the Church in the unjust committal of a man who has done nothing worse than to fall in love, is, in many ways, even more reprehensible. That said, I should point out that Broderick's own experience of priests was not all negative. He was very friendly with the former Professor of English at Maynooth College, Fr Peter Connolly, who was vehemently opposed to the banning of his books in Ireland and who campaigned against their censorship.

Willie reaches some kind of accommodation with his family before the end of the novel by agreeing to attend Mass in his nephew's house. He receives Holy Communion and his family is satisfied with this external sign of piety. They are happy to believe that Willie has seen the error of his ways. However, Fr Mannix is not so sure. He knows that Willie didn't go to Confession before the Mass and that, as such, he has committed a mortal sin. The struggle between them continues long after the family has accepted Willie's return to the fold. They discuss Willie's former lover, Roger, and his apparent reconciliation with the Church. For Willie, the worst sin of all is hypocrisy. He knows that if he had been able to conform more, his life would have been much easier. But he wants Fr Mannix to know the truth about what happened all those years ago. Roger had not given up seeing Willie who couldn't endure his friend going to Mass and Communion on Sundays and making love to him in the dark. In what is one of the high points of the novel, Willie says to Fr Mannix:

> Roger never gave up what you like to call 'vice'. If it's of any interest to you now I never wanted it, not with him anyway. It was he who – how would you put it? – seduced me. Yes, that's how you'd put it. I hated it; but I did it because I loved him.[16]

Whatever criticisms can be leveled at Broderick's writings, it cannot be said that he shied away from addressing issues of a contentious nature. *The Waking of Willie Ryan* is Broderick's best novel in my opinion, as it has a good story-line and is well narrated. He doesn't interfere too much either with his characters' organic growth. While some of Broderick's writings have little to recommend them, others such as *The Pilgrimage* and *The Waking of Willie Ryan* are accomplished works. The highest compliment I can pay him is to say that he is an Irish novelist in the European tradition. He also knows how to spin a good yarn and is able to capture the atmosphere of ennui and social frustration.

I hope that this brief assessment of Broderick's works will highlight him as a writer who, in spite of his many weaknesses, still displays power and courage in addressing issues that were taboo in his time. In my view he owes more to a European, and more specifically French, tradition of challenge and protest than he does to any Irish influence. He did not hesitate to expose the foibles inherent in the Ireland of his time. The year 1999 marked the tenth anniversary of his death and already I sense a change of feeling towards him in Ireland. It's almost as if people are finally beginning to realise that behind the bitter façade was a sad alcoholic man who could never fully gain acceptance for himself in this country and who died an exile in the English town of Bath. He deserves a posthumous acceptance as a writer of merit. Julien Green, writing about *The Pilgrimage*, made the following telling statement:

> In England, as well as in Ireland, the book provoked a scandal. But then again, Ireland has always had her rebellious children. Rebels are almost her speciality and, as is the case in all countries, these are the ones to which she remains most attached, when it is too late. One only has to consider the fate of Joyce, Wilde, Synge and all the others....[17]

I would not like to be accused of overstepping the mark by putting Broderick on a par with the three major Irish writers mentioned above. I agree with Julien Green that he was a rebel, but his rebelliousness had as much to do with his own complex psyche as with any specific Irish trait. As I pointed out at the beginning of the chapter, he was as attached to traditional Catholicism as Evelyn Waugh was. He is very close to the description of the religious man given by Aunt Kate in *The Fugitives*: 'Only the really religious people turn against religion in this country. The ones that are at the top and bottom of every religious organisation are the ones that have no religion at all.'[18] Broderick's rebellion stemmed from how far-removed the Catholic Church of his time was from the glorious image he harboured of it. He loved and hated his native country in equal measure but his decision to end his days in England was an unhappy one because the uprooting left a yawning vacuum in his life. To conclude, one final quotation from *The Fugitives*, which provides a good summary of Broderick's disillusionment and sense of displacement before his death:

> Those who have pulled up their roots have nothing but bleeding stumps with which to explore the no-man's land they inhabit.[19]

NOTES

1. Preface to *Le Pèlerinage* (Editions La Découverte, 1991). The translation is my own. Most of Broderick's novels are available in French translation, which contrasts starkly to the unavailability of the vast majority of his books in Ireland.
2. Patrick Murray's excellent article, 'Athlone's John Broderick', *Éire-Ireland*, Winter 1992, is essential reading for anyone wishing to get to know the writer's oeuvre more intimately. The quote about the Mass is on p. 27.

3. *The Pilgrimage* (London: Weidenfeld and Nicolson, 1961), p. 171.

4. *The Irish Times*, 1 June 1989.

5. Tony Flannery, *From the Inside. A Priest's View of the Catholic Church* (Cork: Mercier Press, 1999), pp. 43-4. Fr Flannery deals at some length also with the hurt and pain caused by *Humanae Vitae* and says that some of the virulent reaction to the recent sexual scandals involving priests in Ireland is a residue of the feelings aroused by the authoritarian Church of the past.

6. 'The Novels of John Broderick', *The Irish Novel in our Time* (eds) Patrick Rafroidi and Maurice Harmon (Lille: PUL, 1976), p. 240.

7. In Julia Carson (ed.), *Banned in Ireland. Censorship and the Irish Writer* (Athens, University of Georgia Press, 1990), p. 46.

8. Ibid., p. 17.

9. *The Fugitives* (London: Weidenfeld and Nicolson, 1962), p. 6.

10. *Don Juaneen* (London: Weidenfeld and Nicolson, 1963), p. 43. The emphasis is my own.

11. *An Apology for Roses* (London: Calder and Boyars, 1973), p. 20.

12. *Moïra* (trans.) Denise Folliot (London: Quartet Books, 1985), p. 163.

13. *The Pride of Summer* (London: Harrap, 1976), pp. 33-4.

14. *An Apology for Roses*, op. cit., p. 52.

15. *The Trial of Fr Dillingham* (London: Abacus, 1982), p. 65.

16. *The Waking of Willie Ryan* (London: Weidenfeld and Nicolson, 1965), pp. 158-9.

17. Preface to the French edition of *The Pilgrimage*, op. cit.

18. *The Fugitives*, op. cit., p. 151.

19. Ibid., p. 135.

8

RELIGION WITHOUT FAITH IN THE
BELFAST NOVELS OF BRIAN MOORE

The novelist Brian Moore (1921-99) is known to a wide international readership. When described by Graham Greene as 'My favourite living novelist', an icon is shaped. However, Moore viewed this accolade as a milestone around his neck and felt pressurised to be different from Greene. His experiments with various literary genres, ranging from the thriller to the psychological novel, to the historical novel remind one of Greene, but when it comes to his treatment of Catholicism, he is very different. Greene had all the fervour of the convert and dealt dramatically with crises of faith in novels like *The Power and the Glory* (1940) and *The Heart of the Matter* (1948). The whiskey-priest in the earlier novel is one of the great portrayals of how an anointed servant of Christ can maintain the mystery of his ministry even when he has fallen into moral decrepitude and succumbed to alcohol. The reader has the impression that, in spite of his sins, this South American priest dies like a saint. We suspect the same outcome for Scobie *(The Heart of the Matter)*, but we are left wondering. A police-officer in the British colonies, Scobie, out of pity and a desire to comfort a helpless woman, enters into an illicit and adulterous relationship with her. His suicide is obviously problematic. The use of sin by God – the *felix culpa* – to allow the cleansing action of grace is a common theme in Greene. This is not true of Moore, as we shall see.

Moore died on 12 January 1999. I remember thinking that one of my favourite writers had completed his life's work. There is a close link, almost a connivance, between Moore and his readers. Hearing him give interviews on radio and television in his gentle, slightly sad Belfast tones, I was always struck by the honesty of his answers, especially those concerning his loss of religious faith. He was born into a middle-class Catholic Belfast family, his father being a well-respected and successful doctor, while his uncle through marriage was Eoin McNeill, one of the leaders of the Easter 1916 uprising. In spite of the fervour of the Moore household, young Moore soon discovered that he 'lacked the religious sense'.[1] His problems began with confession. He doubted that it was necessary to announce his sexual peccadilloes to a stranger. So he began to lie in the confessional and was surprised afterwards at how little fear he experienced of God's retribution. His loss of faith was probably one of the main reasons why he left Belfast in 1942. He realised that living as an agnostic in a God-fearing Ulster society would be an impossible task for him. In a passage from 'The Expatriate Writer' – which is repeated almost word-for-word in *The Emperor of Ice-Cream* (1965) – he describes a departure from Belfast. Having boarded the ferry, which marks the embarking on a new existence, the young emigrant strikes up a conversation with a man who asks him what are his reasons for departing Ireland:

> I'm leaving home because I don't want to be a doctor like my father and brothers. Because I want to be a writer. I want to write.... Perhaps that's the way a lot of people become writers. They don't like the role they're playing and writing seems a better one.[2]

There are autobiographical overtones in these lines but Moore's immediate reason for leaving Belfast in 1942 was his desire to get involved in the war effort. He was disgusted by Ireland's neutrality during World War II and volunteered in a civilian capacity as a non-conscript. Initially serving with the British Ministry of War Transport, his work brought him to North Africa, France and Italy, and he subsequently joined the United Nations, which sent him to Poland (Warsaw). Strangely enough, his first-hand experience of the latter stages of the war never provided fodder for Moore's novels – Greene used similar experiences as background to his novels. From Poland, Moore travelled to Canada, where he worked for three years with the Montreal *Gazette,* before the relative success of *The Lonely Passion of Judith Hearne* (1955) allowed him to concentrate exclusively on creative writing. After the break-up of his first marriage, Moore settled in California with his second wife, Jean. He returned regularly to Ireland to see his mother but after 1942 he was only ever a visitor.

He often admitted his admiration for the French literary tradition. He maintained, and with justification, that the French respect and cherish their writers and intellectuals, something that could not be said of many other countries and especially not of Ireland. He also liked to quote François Mauriac, in particular one of his more famous pronouncements: 'For the novelist, the door closes at twenty.' By this, I presume Mauriac meant that the experiences that mould us are those of childhood and adolescence. That is not to say that novelists don't use the experiences they live through in later years, but that the mould is cast: the characters have been formed, the ethos nourished. When Moore himself began writing, he depended on his childhood memories of Belfast, which came flooding back to him. In *The Lonely Passion of Judith Hearne* (1955) and *The Feast of Lupercal* (1958), he is highly critical of religious hypocrisy – a favourite target of Mauriac's also – and of a repressive Catholic upbringing that imbues an unhealthy distrust of all sexual activity. I should stress, however, that Moore was never anti-Catholic. There was no obvious bitterness towards religion in his writings, rather a sense of loss in people like Judith Hearne, who could not find in religion what she had lost in the struggle for self-respect and recognition as a human being. Judith Hearne and Diarmuid Devine *(The Feast of Lupercal)* live in a kind of Catholic ghetto, mixing only with other Catholics – Devine's problems emerge when he falls in love with Una, a young Protestant from Dublin – and they become acutely aware of the strong connections between faith and nationalist identity. The bitterness of Moore with regard to the education he received in the diocesan school, St Malachy's, is well-documented.[3] He hated school, especially the rote learning and the excessive use of the cane for the slightest misdemeanour. In terms of religious practice, he felt that there was no room allowed for questioning dogmas or for developing personal responsibility for his actions. Fear was the dominant feature of Catholicism as he knew it at that time, fear of eternal damnation and the fires of Hell. Which leads us to the major literary influence on Moore, James Joyce, another spiritual exile:

> In my 20s, before I began to write myself, Joyce was already, for me, the exemplar of what a writer should be: an exile, a rebel, a man willing to endure poverty, discouragement, the hardships of illness, and the misunderstanding of critics, a man who would sacrifice his life to the practice of writing.[4]

He's talking here about a type of spiritual martyrdom for the sake of art. Irish twentieth-century novelists could not avoid looking up to Joyce when setting out on their literary careers. However, they had to be careful not to re-hash what had already been done in such an exemplary fashion by the greatest exponent of Irish fiction. Moore admitted how conscious he was of Joyce when writing his first novel:

> I wanted to write about my own loss of faith, but did not want to risk adverse comparisons with him [Joyce] by describing the loss of faith in a young Irishman. …I decided to write not about an intellectual's loss of faith but of the loss of faith in someone devout, the sort of woman my mother would have known, a 'sodality lady'.[5]

He chose a woman instead – Judith Hearne. The first comment I would like to make in relation to *The Lonely Passion of Judith Hearne* is to stress how utterly dark and decrepit the pervading atmosphere is. There is no hope, no light to brighten or alleviate the suffering of the main character. The first pages of the novel see the heroine, a spinster music teacher, moving in to new digs. The worn carpet and poor general upkeep of the house reveals to the reader that this is not at all the kind of place where you'd find socially ambitious lodgers. Her painstaking ritual of unpacking – the placing of 'dear aunt's photograph in the exact middle of the mantelpiece'[6] and the hanging of the coloured oleograph of the Sacred Heart at the head of the bed – reveals the importance of religion and family in Judith's hierarchy of values. The landlady's son, Bernard Rice, 'stared at Miss Hearne with bloodshot eyes, rejecting her as all males had before him' (*Judith Hearne*, p. 10). It is thus evident that her single status – emphasised by the 'Miss Hearne' in the narrative – is imputable to a singular lack of beauty and an absence of material possessions. This latter point is overlooked by James Madden, Mrs Rice's brother, recently returned from the United States, who is anxious to find a suitable (preferably well-off) wife and settle down in Ireland:

> He smiles at her. Friendly, she is. And educated. Those
> rings and that gold wrist-watch. They're real. A pity she
> looks like that. (p. 39)

Madden's inability to see Judith's relative poverty is matched
by Judith's romantic imaginings of a life with this 'Yankee'
widower. The reader's insights are clearer than either of their's
and it is immediately obvious that tragedy is looming. Madden
is a drunkard and a sexual deviant – the flogging and
subsequent rape carried out by him on the servant girl, Mary, a
minor, illustrate this and reveal the fallaciousness of Judith's rosy
image of him. His wish is to profit from his sister's tenant's
illusory wealth. Judith equally has a problem with alcohol, and
seeks escape from her miserable existence through bouts of
heavy drinking in her room – we get the impression that her
recent change of digs might be attributable to this problem.
Before beginning what she views as a sinful act (the abuse of
alcohol), she turns the Sacred Heart towards the wall. But she
cannot avoid sensing his disapproval:

> He looked at her, stern now, warning that this might be
> her last chance ever and that He might become the Stern
> Judge before morning came, summoning her to that
> terrible final accounting. (p. 112)

Judith's impression of God is that of a very authoritarian and
censorious judge who is constantly on the look out for
weaknesses in his creatures. At no point does she receive any
comfort from religion, as is revealed in the following lines:

> Religion was there: it was not something you thought
> about, and if, occasionally, you had a small doubt about
> something in the way church affairs were carried on, or

> something that seemed wrong or silly, well, that was the
> devil at work and God's ways were not our ways. You
> could pray for guidance. (p. 67)

This unthinking compliance to laws and regulations seems commonplace in Judith Hearne's world. Attendance at Mass, receiving the sacraments, external observance of Catholic mores, are what characterise religion in her milieu. James Madden thinks nothing of going to Mass after raping Mary and is not in any visible way upset or guilty about his action. Fr Quigley berates his congregation during a sermon for not finding time for God, while he himself is dismissive of Judith's self-confessed crisis of faith when she goes to him for spiritual guidance. He dispenses with her quickly so that he can away to the golf club. He does not see the contradiction between the words of his sermon and his abandoning of a woman in need. Judith is left in a state of despair; alone, unloved, without faith in a higher being. Yet she turns to the Sacred Heart for help:

> O Sacred Heart, please, I need Your strength, Your help.
> Why should life be so hard for me, why am I alone, why
> did I yield to the temptation of drink, why, why has it all
> happened like this? (p. 139)

Judith's prayers go unanswered. She looks hard at the tabernacle and comes to the conclusion that 'there was no God. Only round wagers of unleavened bread' (p. 140). And if that is the case, what has been the purpose of her life? What has been the point of the sacrifices she has made in the name of religion? Why did she worry so much about committing sin if there was nobody watching over her? Bernard Rice, ever a friend to the needy, asks Judith: 'Why are you alone tonight, if it isn't for your silly religious scruples?'(p. 182), and adds: 'Your God is only a picture on the wall. He doesn't give a damn about you' (p. 183). Bernard is unfeeling and selfish but he is also a keen judge of character. He sees the pathetic attempts that Judith makes to maintain a certain respectability that has long since deserted her. Her Sunday visits to the O'Neills, who dread her arrival but who don't know how to put her off coming, are the highlight of her week. The O'Neill's are wealthy and seemingly intelligent – Mr O'Neill is a university professor – and endure Judith out of religious obligation. As usual, she misreads the signs and thinks that the visits are as important to the O'Neill's as they are to her. One Sunday afternoon she overindulges in sherry and becomes inebriated. Mrs O'Neill is outraged, an emotion that is further heightened when Miss Hearne arrives unannounced – and drunk – in the middle of the week to elaborate on her religious problems:

> God! Miss Hearne said bitterly. What does *He* care? Is there a God at all, I've been asking myself, because if there is, why does He never answer our prayers? Why does He allow all these things to happen? Why? (p. 229)

Bereft of suitors, condemned to a life on her own, without the comfort of friends and religion, Judith, in desperation, turns to the 'bottle', in the hope of finding 'the key to contentment' (p. 113). She drinks to flee from oppressive reality, in order to view her trials more philosophically. But she wakes to find that her problems, instead of disappearing, have, if anything, intensified. All the props that supported the fiction that her life was bearable, tumble down around her. Faced with the sordid reality of her existence, with her increasing dependence on alcohol, with the true feelings James Madden has towards her, she has a nervous breakdown. The novel ends with her in a convalescence home, where her only visitors are Fr Quigley and Mrs O'Neill.

The Lonely Passion of Judith Hearne is the best novel that Moore wrote but it makes depressing reading. Its realism and raw honesty are a compelling mix, as is the detached narrative, which never falls into the trap of didacticism. Then there is Moore's capacity to enter the mind of his heroine, which is remarkable. We suffer through all her humiliations and pain, the shattering of her illusions about herself and life in general. Her faith, which has no intellectual basis, fails her in her hour of greatest need. Denis Sampson offers this excellent assessment of the novel:

> The collapse of Judith Hearne's faith is accompanied by a recognition that all along she has concealed from herself her essential loneliness, and that, just as she has been free to fantasise, she is equally free to rebel against the hypocritical conformity that has repressed her freedom for herself. Hers is a desperate, drunken and failed rebellion, and, in Moore's view, that is true to the way most rebellions are aborted in life.[7]

This is clearly a novel of despair, where the God of Repression replaces the God of Hope and Love. The ultimate irony, according to Sampson,[8] is that a novel that depicts so truthfully the repressive climate of Catholic, nationalist Belfast, should have been banned for indecency in the Republic by the Irish Censorship Board, an institution seeking to ensure a similar climate on this side of the border.

The Feast of Lupercal is ultimately more critical of religion, but religion here is mainly a social umbrella – even more superficial than Judith's. Diarmuid Devine, an English teacher in the Catholic Belfast school, Ardath,[9] is upset one day to overhear two of his colleagues refer to him as an 'old maid'. He wonders if there mightn't be some truth in their opinion of him.

Thirty-seven years of age, a bachelor, with no obvious attributes apart from a capacity to anticipate exam questions for his students and to organise the local drama group, he begins a self-examination. From being indifferent as to whether or not he ever entered into a serious relationship with a woman, he starts to cultivate female company. A colleague, Tim Heron, invites him to his house to mark the occasion of his daughter's engagement, and there he encounters Heron's niece, Una, a Protestant from Dublin. Dev's reaction to his discovery that he has actually met a Protestant captures the type of stereotypical reaction of his tribe:

> Protestants were the hostile Establishment, leaders with Scots and English surnames, hard, blunt businessmen who asked what school you went to and, on hearing your answer, refused the job.... To them, Catholics were a hated minority, a minority who threatened their rule.[10]

More importantly, given his desire to broaden his sexual horizons, Protestant girls were generally known to be *fast*. As if to prove this particular thesis, Devine discovers that Una has been forced by her parents to leave Dublin because she had been 'carrying on' with a married man. When he is asked by Fr McSwiney to resurrect a cast for a play he previously directed to raise funds for a charitable cause, Devine decides that Una might be a suitable choice for the leading female role. Private tuition sessions follow and he falls in love. It's a dangerous dream that they might end up together, given their differing religious backgrounds and the forces that are working against them. Dev is aware that he is in danger of alienating his employers by being seen publicly in Una's company:

> Man was born sinful, he must avoid the occasions of sin. The men who ran Ardath did not believe in words of

> honour, they did not consider human intention a match
> for the devil's lures. (*The Feast of Lupercal*, p. 79)

He is 'playing with fire' but, consumed with passion, he cannot bring himself to avoid further emotional involvement. New clothes and an improved general appearance bear witness to a man out to impress a young lady. He takes dancing lessons to prepare for the dreaded night when Una might want to attend a dance in his company – he is awkward and clumsy on the floor. Moore builds up the tension very effectively as we wait for events to take their course. Sure enough, after having been turned down for the main part in the play – mainly as a result of the covert machinations of Fr McSwiney – Una asks to be brought out the following night. The dance floor brings them closer and afterwards Una asks to be brought back to Dev's digs where, to his horror, he finds that she is prepared to offer herself to him. This is not what he wants; he is incapable of going through with it:

> In this, his own solitary bed where he had sinned a
> thousand times in sinful imaginings, repented nightly in
> mumbled acts of contrition, in this bed this very night,
> real sin would be consummated. There was no getting
> out of it. She would be here in a moment. (p. 144)

Devine's shock and fear are obvious to Una, who looks on his reaction to her naked body as a rejection. Upset and confused, she falls asleep in the flat – she is half-drunk anyway – and is caught entering her uncle's house the next morning. The worst is suspected: Devine and she have slept together. Tim Heron ends up caning his colleague in front of the Priests' House and they are both brought to explain themselves to the headmaster, Dr Keogh, in his office. Dr Keogh is one of the only positive portrayals of a priest-character in Moore's early work. He does not automatically view his English teacher's actions in the worst possible light and urges him to explain what actually transpired between himself and the young lady on the night in question. He accepts the explanation and, contrary to the wishes of his dean, Fr McSwiney, decides not to dismiss either Heron or Devine. The overall portrayal of Catholicism in this novel is once more a very negative one. When thinking about his travails with Una, Devine notes:

> If I had been a Protestant, this would never have happened, he thought. I would have had my fill of girls by now. I would never have had to go to confession. (p. 212)

There is far less reference to Devine's feelings about religion than there is to Judith Hearne's. The social pressures of his position as a teacher in a Catholic school are what Moore dwells on. Devine is less pathetic than Judith. He has reasonable economic independence and does at least exert some power in the classroom. He doesn't think too much about questions of faith but becomes aware of how powerful his Catholic upbringing has been when he confronts the danger of committing a mortal sin with Una. He cannot go through with it; he cannot forget what he is about to do. I don't in any way feel that this in itself is a negative – in fact, it has the one very positive effect of ensuring the hero's continued employment in Ardath – but there is a marked impression given in the novel that fornication is a social taboo. Tim Heron cannot discuss the matter without yielding to blind violence and Fr McSwiney is inclined to similar sentiments. The crude poems written by some pupils about Devine and Una on the toilet walls in the school display a warped attitude to sexuality. The hero is aware that he has no real choice about his religion and recognises that it has had many drawbacks for his personal development. In relation to the portrayal of religion in the two novels with which we are dealing, Jo O'Donoghue makes this observation:

> For the two main protagonists, Judith Hearne and Diarmuid Devine, religion is not a choice, not a gift, not in any sense a joy or a blessing. It has been imposed on them, with all its devotions, its limitations and its prejudices, by their families and their backgrounds. Their belief is not really a belief at all because they only observe their religion by default.[11]

This is a fair summation of Moore's treatment of religious belief in the early Belfast novels. An examination of later novels such as *I am Mary Dunne* (1968) and *The Temptation of Eileen Hughes* (1981) show how Moore came to see the futility of the secular gods, money and sex for example, to whom his characters turn in an attempt to find a replacement for religious belief. Devine's attitude to religion is different to that of Judith. He is not a person of deep religious convictions: he is a victim of compliance to the demands of his job and of his presumed role and behaviour in society. He is weak and he suffers, but never turns to God for help with his difficulties. Therefore, he doesn't suffer from the same sense of divine rejection as Judith.

Although he was never a practising Catholic after he left Belfast, Moore held on to a fascination with religious belief that would always stay with him. In a letter which Denis Sampson quotes in his book, Moore wrote:

> ...while I left the Church, I've always had a very strong interest in Catholicism. I've felt as a writer that man's search for a faith, whether it is within the Catholic Church or a belief in God or a belief in something other than merely the materialistic world, is a major theme.[12]

These lines encapsulate the attitude of Moore to faith. Sometimes he appears to be buying into the Joycean popular religion of art and at other times he seems to be genuinely fascinated with characters who have real faith, which he never found in his own life. The two novels we have looked at illustrate a negative portrayal of religion as lived out by two hapless characters in the dark and oppressive atmosphere of Belfast, a city that has been witness to far too much sectarian hatred and violence. Judith and Devine are trapped in the past, especially in a religious past that has hardly changed in two centuries, and desperately seek the freedom to choose a new life. Their helplessness, however, is just as obvious at the end of the novels as it was in the beginning. In an interview with journalist Joe O'Connor, Moore stated: 'Belief is an obsession of mine. I think that everybody wants to believe in something – politics, religion, something that makes life worthwhile for them. And with most people there's a certain point in their lives – usually in their thirties – when these beliefs are shattered. And it's that point I seize on as a writer.'[13] Judith Hearne and Diarmuid Devine are two good examples of how meaningless life becomes when belief is taken from them and when religious practice is shown to be bereft of faith.

Maybe Mauriac was right in saying that for the novelist the door closes at twenty. Genes, education, family, religion and society shape and mould physical, mental and moral attitudes, which neither a Joyce nor a Moore nor a Mauriac nor a Bernanos could discard. They thus transformed them into literary treasures that illuminate the vistas of humanity.

NOTES

1. The quote is from an interview Moore did for the BBC in 1997 with Róisín McAuley.
2. 'The Expatriate Writer', in *The Antigonish Review*, 17, Spring 1974, pp. 28-9.
3. In Julia Carson's *Banned in Ireland. Censorship and the Irish Writer* (Athens: University of Georgia Press, 1990), p. 111, he stated: 'I went to St Malachy's, which was the only Catholic boarding school in Belfast at the time. It was a terrible school. I would say that the most serious effect of censorship that I can think of in Ireland doesn't start with book banning: it started, in my day, with the books chosen by Catholic institutions.'
4. Quoted by Denis Sampson, *Brian Moore: the Chameleon Novelist* (Dublin: Marino, 1998), p. 86. This is a very good reference when it comes to understanding Moore the man and writer.
5. Quoted by D. Sampson, op. cit., p. 88.
6. *The Lonely Passion of Judith Hearne* (London: Flamingo, 1994), p. 7. All my references will be to this edition of the novel.
7. D. Sampson, *Brian Moore*, op. cit., p. 96.
8. Ibid., p. 105.
9. Ardath is commonly accepted as being a thinly disguised representation of St Malachy's.
10. *The Feast of Lupercal* (London: Granada Publishing, 1983), p. 35.
11. Jo O'Donoghue, *Brian Moore: a Critical Study* (McGill-Queen's University Press, 1991), p. 60. This book is an indispensable reference for anyone wishing to appreciate Moore's main themes and his novelistic craftsmanship.
12. In Denis Sampson, op. cit., p. 210.
13. *The Sunday Tribune*, 1 October 1995.

9

JOHN McGAHERN, A WRITER IN TUNE WITH HIS TIME

John McGahern was born in Dublin on 12 November 1934, but soon after his birth the family moved to Ballinamore in the small western county of Leitrim. From such simple beginnings he grew into one of our foremost living Irish novelists. This is not a claim that is made without due consideration, for Ireland is a country where poets and novelists are as plentiful as they are talented. One of the attributes that distinguishes McGahern from other contemporary Irish novelists is his unique ability to capture in a poetic way the lives of rural families in the west of Ireland in the forties and fifties. For people who wish to get an insight into this close-knit, religious and sometimes violent race, there is no better reference than the writings of McGahern. He has often paid the price for his frank portrayal of the society within which he was reared and which he constantly mines for his artistic inspiration. His second novel, *The Dark*, published in 1965, was immediately banned in Ireland and was partially responsible for his dismissal from his teaching position. He deals with this episode in the semi-autobiographical novel, *The Leavetaking* (1974), in which the soon-to-be-sacked national school teacher notes:

> If I applied to go on the higher [salary] scale the authorities would discover that I wasn't properly married.

> If I remained on the single salary, which I'd have to do, they'd find out sooner or later in such a small city that I was living as a married man but not married. Either way I was certain to be fired. All education in Ireland was denominational. While the State paid teachers, it was the Church who hired and fired.[1]

Not only was McGahern a writer, but he had also been married in a Registry Office. The Catholic Church, which almost completely controlled Irish education at the time, did not tolerate such behaviour from its teachers, even very talented ones like McGahern. Censorship extended to many walks of life. After his dismissal, McGahern went to live in London for a time but returned to a small farm that he bought in Leitrim in 1974. He still lives there.

There seems to be a tradition of exile among Irish novelists from the time of Joyce. In his fine article, 'Inherited Dissent',[2] Augustine Martin remarked: 'The relations between the Irish artist and his society have been strained since our literature emerged from the nineteenth century.' He explains this tension by an examination of the literary tradition that the artists inherited and the environment or society in which they found themselves. In relation to the former point, there can be no doubt that the shadow of Joyce and Yeats weighed heavily on all Irish writers in the twentieth century. With such predecessors as these, it was always going to be difficult to find an unused path. Consciously or unconsciously, Irish writers had inherited a certain image of the artist in exile, punished for his art by an unfeeling and unappreciative public. This is particularly strong in Joyce, who in many ways cultivated and exaggerated the stereotype of the exiled writer. When one adds to this a society in which the Catholic Church was still a dominant and, in some ways, a repressive force, the full extent of the conflict can be better gauged. Because of the artist's role in depicting the human passions, it is inevitable in many ways that there will be friction when it comes to the artist's portrayal of sexual and moral issues. François Mauriac, a devout Catholic, received a hostile response to his novels among many traditional Catholics in France who found it difficult to accept his depiction of the hypocrisy of many *bien-pensant* co-religionists. In Ireland, the situation confronting a novelist like McGahern was at times even more perilous. Any perceived slight on the Catholic religion was poorly received in a country where Catholicism and national identity were so closely linked. In our struggle for political hegemony it was our Catholicism that distinguished us from the colonising British and from the Protestant ascendancy in our own country, who remained largely loyal to the British Crown. The French had a long history of questioning external control of their religious practices; they also had the philosophical formation to deal with problems of a metaphysical nature. The Irish were poorly equipped to think issues through for themselves. They were happy in general to allow a powerful secular clergy do their thinking for them. Being mainly a rural society, they were attached to their rituals. Irish society today probably still lacks the philosophical basis that enables the French to believe even when they are professedly atheistic.

McGahern is the pitiless chronicler of a closed Irish society which was recovering from the end of British rule and which was trying to come to terms with the reality of living in an independent Republic. Many of his male characters, Reegan in *The Barracks* (1963) and Moran in *Amongst Women* (1990), are veterans of the War of Independence. Both feel bitter at what has been the outcome of their struggle for freedom; the society that independence has spawned does not impress them and they consider themselves to be forgotten and unappreciated, somewhat like the artist. In this short critique, I illustrate the manner in which McGahern captures some essential aspects of the society in which he grew up and I make the case that his novels are worthy of careful scrutiny for both their literary and their cultural values. Just as Balzac capures many quintessential elements of French society in the first half of the nineteenth century, so McGahern is an essential reference for someone wishing to infiltrate the rural and religious landscape in the Ireland of the forties and fifties. I will limit my treatment to the writer's first novel, *The Barracks* (1963), and his most recent one, *Amongst Women* (1990), to show a consistency and, at the same time, an evolution in McGahern's thinking.

The compelling and haunting presence of Elizabeth Reegan is what principally makes *The Barracks* such a moving first novel. There is much to admire in this view of a small rural community as seen through the eyes of the wife of the local sergeant. As is the case of Rose in *Amongst Women*, Elizabeth marries a widower with a young family and inherits the domestic and emotional responsibilities of the household. Her husband feels trapped in a job that gives him no satisfaction and no hope. His daily routine is monotonous and he is in constant battle with his superintendent, Quirke, for whom he has scant respect and whom he seeks to undermine at every opportunity. Elizabeth is the main focus of the novel and we see almost everything through her eyes. One cold and wet evening, after he has completed his rounds, her husband turns on the radio at the end of the Sweepstake programme (a type of National Lottery of the time) and she hears intoned the words of the song: 'It makes no difference who you are, you can wish upon a star.' Her whole existence seems to be summed up in her reaction to this cliché:

> It should all make you want to cry. You were lonely. The night was dark and deep. You must have some wish or

longing. The life you lead, the nine to five at the office, the drudgery of a farm, the daily round, cannot be endured without hope.[3]

She speaks in soliloquies, unburdening herself to herself. She has little reason to be hopeful. She feels the cancerous cysts growing in her breasts, senses the dissatisfaction of her husband and the humdrum routine of her life. It is difficult to find the strength to go on living. McGahern is particuarly adept at painting the capacity of a certain human breed to persevere in the face of the most intense adversity, namely the survivors. Elizabeth is subjected to much physical and emotional torture and yet she keeps her routine going. She gets up early, lights the fire, prepares the breakfast, gets the kids out to school, exchanges pleasantries with her husband and succeeds in blotting out her forebodings. The dangerous moments come when she has a few minutes to relax:

> The starkness of individual minutes passing through accidental doors and windows and chairs and flowers and trees, cigarette smoke or the light growing brilliant and fading losing their pain, gathered into oneness in the vision of her whole life passing in its total mystery. A girl child growing up on a small farm, the blood of puberty, the shock of the first sexual act, the long years in London, her marriage back into this enclosed place happening as would her death in moments where cigarettes were smoked. No one, not even herself, could measure it by slide or rule. (p. 59)

This process of 'involuntary memory', made famous by Proust, is evident here. The essence of her life is captured in uncontrolled moments of intense revelation, reduced to its bare essentials. You are born, grow some and then die. The cycle is inexorable. In spite of the drudgery of her daily chores, Elizabeth clings to life, sees the beauty of nature, relives the happy moments she has enjoyed. She knows that her husband has remained a stranger to her, that there has never been any real understanding between them. As in most of McGahern's depictions of married couples, the Reegans enjoy little intimacy other than the occasional physical coupling. Their relationship is probably typical of many marriages of the time in Ireland. Unions were made and consummated without the frills of romance. The men worked, while the women stayed at home, did the housework, catered for their families' needs. There wasn't any time for deep conversations. Life imposed too many demands for idle talk to interfere with routine. The sounds of the barracks, the guards coming and going, the change of the seasons, the meals eaten together, the beauty of nature, all these elements are brought together marvellously in the heroine's reveries. When Elizabeth knows she is dying, the harsh realisation that she will soon leave this world strikes her with primeval force:

> It was so beautiful when she let the blinds up first thing that, 'Jesus Christ', softly was all she was able to articulate as she looked out and up the river to the woods across the lake, black with the leaves fallen except the red rust of the beech trees, the withered reeds standing pale and sharp as bamboo rods at the edges of the water, the fields of the hill always white and the radio aerial that went across from the window to the high branches of the sycamore a pure white line through the air. (p. 170)

This familiar scene of which up until now she has never really taken any notice, is suddenly etched on her consciousness. She realises she is soon to leave her surroundings, and she is sad.

The power of her description of a standard rural Irish scene heightens our awareness of what joy life can bring even in the most unpromising situations, what sadness also. The moments of perception we share with Elizabeth are poignant. We feel her physical pain, her fatigue, her anguish, her awe at the beauty of nature. The novelist succeeds in involving us intimately in her fate, a fine artistic achievement. We share her recollections of the time she spent nursing in London, her affair with a doctor, Halliday, a man with scant regard for polite circles, who is bedevilled by a steadfast belief in the absurdity of the human condition. The affair ended sadly; Halliday couldn't bear to impose his angst on Elizabeth and terminated the relationship before she could be contaminated by his darkness. At least, this is the reason he gave Elizabeth; his real motivation was more complex. The adventure had served its purpose, in any case, because Elizabeth had at least come to see another side to life. She realised that it wasn't always necessary to accept blindly the belief system that was handed down to her. Halliday challenged all accepted truths, encouraged Elizabeth to do likewise. This is perhaps the reason why she adopts such an independent line when the parish priest attempts to enlist her services for the local branch of the Legion of Mary: '…a kind of legalized gossiping school to the women and a convenient pool of labour that the priests could draw on for catering committees' (p. 163). She rejects his overtures, a brave course for a woman at that time.

The presence of religion is constant in the novel. The Rosary at night, Mass and the sacraments, these all form part of the daily routine. People who chose not to practise their religion are held in deep distrust. Even Reegan's lack of respect for his superior officer does not extend to challenging the Church's teaching.[4] He intones his grievances against Quirke, while being largely unaware of the illness of his wife, her worry:

> She was quiet. Nothing short of a miracle would change any of their lives, their lives and his life and her life without purpose, and it seemed as if it might never come now, she changed his words in her own mind but she did not speak. (p. 174)

Elizabeth Reegan is a symbol of many of the distinctive qualities of Irish women. She has great inner strength, a capacity to suffer in silence. Her husband needs to unburden himself of his problems. She is the stronger of the two, the more resourceful. She accepts the limits of her existence, does not ask for the impossible. Reegan throws himself into work in the bog so as not to have to face up to the reality of his wife's illness. He does not wish to share in her dying, while she has accepted her fate from an early stage:

> It seemed as a person grew older that the unknowable reality, God, was the one thing that you could believe or disbelieve in with safety, it met you with imponderable silence and could never be reduced to the nothingness of certain knowledge. (p. 177)

That was her type of religion. It gave her no cosy solutions, no convictions about an all-loving God. Her beliefs obviously help her to die with dignity and courage. The death of his wife leaves Reegan in a state of cold resignation. He neglects his duties and waits for the inevitable showdown with Quirke. He feels that he has nothing to lose now and he is determined to relish their final confrontation. His is the ultimate victory as he succeeds in totally overcoming his superior. He had been in a position of power during the War of Independence, and had acquired the habit of being obeyed. He leaves Quirke in no doubt about the differences of their respective positions by telling the superintendent that he wore a uniform during the War of Independence to command men and not just as a means of attempting to earn a respect that isn't merited. The frustration of years of subservience to a man he couldn't respect comes to the boil in this encounter, of which there is only one possible winner. This is Reegan's high point, a type of compensation for the cowardice he had shown during his wife's illness. It is a shallow victory, the conquest of a small mind over a smaller one.

McGahern's first novel gives us then a microcosm of Irish society in the forties. We are put in contact with the daily grind of life, the hopes and aspirations of people, their courage and cowardice, their religious practices, their inertia. The picture is not completely bleak, however. There are some, though not many, shades of hope. Material poverty is matched by a spiritual void; solitude is the norm. When Elizabeth exclaims 'Jesus Christ' at the beauty of this world, however, she is acknowledging that there are moments of joy in the midst of the suffering. Towards the end of the novel we read:

> Outside the morning was clean and cold, men after hot breakfasts were on their way to work. The noises of the morning rose within her to a call of wild excitement. Never had she felt it so when she was rising to let up the blinds in the kitchen and rake out the coals to get their breakfasts, the drag and burden of their lives together was how she'd mostly felt it then, and now it was a wild call to life, life, life and life at any cost. (pp. 201-2)

On the threshold of death, she has a hunger for life like she has never known before. She wants to soak in all the poetry around her before she enters eternity. At times we live without being aware of the beauty that is at the heart of existence. When

Elizabeth comes to appreciate how much happiness she has known in spite of all her pain and suffering in this life, she is already on the point of leaving it all behind.

Amongst Women deals with many similar themes. This time the central interest is a man, Moran, another army veteran who, after the military war is over, continues his reign of terror within the confines of his own home. He is a man with very definite ideas about religion, the family, the land, who cannot bear to be contradicted or undermined in any way. He is a far less sympathetic character than Elizabeth. Ten years elapsed between these novels: the years have deepened McGahern's thinking and honed his craft. This is a novel of substance; the powerful writing resonates with the personal experience of the writer. It was short-listed for the Booker Prize and was heaped with generous critical acclaim. It is clear that Moran is a character who frightens and, at the same time, fascinates McGahern. He has a universal quality that goes way beyond the narrow rural setting in which the novel is set. Denis Sampson captures the essence of *Amongst Women* when he writes: 'Certainly, McGahern has written a novel of family that resonates across cultures.'[5] There is a sense in which the migrant Irish, with rural roots, love to cast a nostalgic glance back towards the 'auld sod'. This novel shows that this romantic nostalgia loses sight of the pain and suffering still flourishing in rural Ireland. Moran's daughters return regularly to visit their father and their stepmother:

> No matter how far in talk the sisters ventured, they kept returning, as if to a magnet, to what Daddy would like or dislike, approve or disapprove of. His unpredictable violences they discounted simply as they might the tantrums of a difficult child.[6]

It is as if their father's innate sense of his own uniqueness and that of the family confers on the daughters a feeling of importance that they only enjoy in their home, the Great Meadow. The fear of a verbal or physical lashing is forgotten and forgiven in the warmth of complicity with which they and Rose, his wife, build up an attractive image of the father figure. They all strive to keep the focal point of the family happy at all costs. The boys, Luke and Michael, are different. Luke leaves home under a cloud, never to return.[7] When his sisters pester him to visit their father before he dies, Luke makes the comment that 'only women could live with Daddy'. Certainly, the tendency to challenge openly parental authority, more prevalent in sons, can have grave consequences. Michael sees his father stare in the direction of his shotgun after the two of them have a brief but serious scuffle. So terrified is he at the prospect of his father reverting to his wartime killing, that he flees the house. The enmity between the younger son and his father is not nearly so strong. This may be in part due to the feminine side of Michael's nature and the protection he received from his sisters and Rose as he was growing up. Moran is desperately keen to hear news of his first-born each time someone returns from a visit to London. This is the offspring that has escaped from his sphere of influence, the one he cannot control. Luke says:

> I didn't choose my father. He didn't choose me. If I'd known, I certainly would have refused to meet the man. No doubt he'd have done likewise with me. (p. 144)

An unlikely theory, especially when applied to a man for whom family values are sacrosanct. His repeated statement that all his children are equal in his eyes is genuine, as is his belief in the maxim: 'The family that prays together stays together.' His use of religion as another means of asserting his authority is seen in the nightly reciting of the Rosary. Each member of the family has a decade, Moran being the person who begins and ends the ritual. His religious quest is an unusual one, as Denis Sampson points out:

> Moran is a disillusioned hero, a man of faith (first in his vocation for the priesthood, then in his vocation of revolutionary fighter) who has lost all faith except a belief in his fiction of 'the family', 'the house'.[8]

This is how McGahern sees religion in Ireland – ritualised, tyrannical, loveless, almost soulless. But he is too good an artist to be pedantic or dogmatic. Moran's disillusionment is illustrated by the last time that his friend, McQuaid, who had served in Moran's squadron in the War of Independence, came to the Great Meadow to celebrate Monaghan Day. This was an annual meeting and one to which Moran attached great importance. The two veterans would talk of the war, eat their fill, attended to by the daughters. On this occasion, McQuaid grew irritated at his friend's compulsion to dominate, to have everything on his own terms or not at all. So he broke the tradition of staying the night, and stood up to leave. Moran realised the consequences of this, the loss of one of the few friendships he held dear, but he could not bring himself to say the words that would diffuse the tension. As McQuaid got into his car he heard the words: 'Some people cannot bear to come in second' (p. 22). The contrast between McQuaid, who has become rich as a cattle-dealer, and Moran, a modest farmer, was difficult to swallow for the latter who had been a commander in the army. On a human level he regretted this dispute:

> After years he had lost his oldest and dearest friend but in a way he had always despised friendship; families were

what mattered, more particularly that larger version of himself, *his* family; and while seated in the same scheming fury he saw each individual member slipping out of his reach. Yes, they would eventually all go. He would be alone. (p. 22)

The children might all leave in geographical terms, but all the daughters will never be fully absent from their birthplace. Maggie will return home regularly from London, even after her marriage. Similarly, Mona and Sheila will religiously make the trip home from Dublin. These trips are what give their lives a focus and a meaning. After a day working together saving hay, when the family functioned as a genuine unit, the love the daughters feel for their father is obvious:

> As they walked away through the greenness, the pale blue above them, Maggie said, her voice thick with emotion, 'Daddy is just lovely when he's like that.' 'There's nobody who can hold a candle to him', Mona added. The girls in their different ways wanted to gather their father and the whole, true, heartbreaking day into their arms. (p. 81)

There is a universal quality in this novel that gives it much more than a local or regional appeal. Each of us has felt love and antipathy for our father, a hunger for the reassurance that being loved by him brings. The struggles that are at the heart of all families are wonderfully captured by McGahern. We are enthralled by his descriptions of the days spent working in the fields, the feverish studying for exams, the process of growing towards independence, the moments of revolt, the pain of uprooting. Foreign readers can relate to the atmosphere of the book, which has a strong Irish flavour but which is at the same time an account of family life that transcends all borders.

McGahern's control of style has tightened over the years. This leaves him freer to project his own vision of life through his characters. He is not a lover of dialogue, preferring the interior monologue that he uses freely to get behind the masks of daily intercourse. What we see behind the masks is what makes his people memorable, not what they say or do. We've had a prolixity of writers telling us about the beauties of the Irish countryside. Their accounts are at times mawkish, romantic or exaggerated. McGahern sees the countryside as part of people's lives – saving the hay, cutting the corn, working in the bog. But he doesn't allow this to interfere with his narrative; it just forms a background, a sort of vision sometimes ignored but then suddenly glimpsed as a revelation. He does not associate such experiences with any divine order. No, they just come to people and make life a little more bearable. But Nature is a mighty force behind the lives of his characters.

His style has developed into a free flow of simple words full of meaning. In *Amongst Women* it has the ease and assurance of a master-novelist. Apart from the style, an important aspect of the evolution is the presentation of the main protagonists. Moran is not as well-developed a character as Elizabeth; he is more of a stereotypical depiction of the domineering father. She is more memorable because more human, more suffering than Moran. We see the latter mainly through the family's eye rather than through insights gleaned from within himself.

This short analysis of McGahern's work may stimulate your interest in a novelist of genuine stature who scrutinises the structures of Irish society – the family, the land, the Catholic religion – and who demonstrates how all three are indelibly ingrained on the Irish psyche. The Irish literary landscape is not simply the domain of Joyce, Beckett, Yeats and, more recently, Heaney. A novelist of McGahern's stature deserves to figure among the best Ireland has to offer. He is someone who paid the price for daring to expose the foibles of the society into which he was born. Like many artists, he found himself on the outside of a Catholic-dominated world, which had an insular mentality. But, instead of conforming, he chose to persevere and to become the chronicler of the modern Ireland which began after the signing of the Truce. His Ireland is not a bright or optimistic place; it doesn't conform to the image many foreigners have of our country. His characters are often prisoners of an oppressive and domineering father or husband, of a rural society that is dangerously conservative and inward-looking and in which the Catholic Church is a repressive force. Given his experience of censorship and exile, it is surprising how little bitterness there is in McGahern's writing. What we hold on to after finishing one of his novels is a strong sense of what it was like to live in rural Ireland a few decades ago and an appreciation of the poetry and vision that make his prose so rewarding. Perhaps the best way to understand the Irish psyche is to immerse ourselves in the writings of someone like McGahern. It is not just the great events of history that forge the mentality of a race, as he has so vividly demonstrated. Often it is, in Wordsworth's words: 'the little nameless unremembered acts/of kindness and of love', combined with equally nameless acts of cruelty and hate, which make us what we are.

NOTES

1. *The Leavetaking*, 2nd edition (Faber & Faber, 1984), p. 142.
2. Augustine Martin, 'Inherited Dissent: the Dilemma of the Irish writer', *Studies*, Spring 1965.
3. *The Barracks* (London: Faber & Faber, 1963), p. 32.
4. 'He'd have none of the big questions: What do you think of life or the relationships between people or any of the other things that have no real answers? He trusted all that to the priests as he trusted a sick body to the doctors and kept whatever observances were laid down as long as they didn't clash with his own passions' (pp. 64-5).
5. Denis Sampson, *Outstaring Nature's Eye. The Fiction of John McGahern* (Washington: Catholic University of America Press, 1993), p. 231. This is an indispensable reference for anyone wishing to understand better the writings of McGahern.
6. *Amongst Women* (London, Faber & Faber, 1990), p. 131.
7. Michael refers to one incident that sums up the relationship between his father and brother: 'Once he made Luke take off all his clothes in the room. We heard the sound of the beating' (p. 113). The violence is never far from the surface. Shortly after her marriage to Moran, Rose notices how ill at ease the children are at times: 'Only when they dropped or rattled something, the startled way they would look towards Moran, did the nervous tension of what it took to glide about so silently show' (p. 53).
8. *Outstaring Nature's Eye*, p. 238.

10

NO CHURCH FOR THE POOR: FRANK McCOURT'S *ANGELA'S ASHES*

Born in Brooklyn in 1930, Frank McCourt moved with his family to Ireland when he was four years of age. He returned to the United States fifteen years later. His first book, *Angela's Ashes*, published in 1996, is a *tour de force* of confessional writing. It has evoked much reaction, some hostile – especially in McCourt's native Limerick, where some people consider his account exaggerated and unjust. It won for its author the prestigious Pulitzer Prize and was voted book of the year by *Time* magazine. Alan Parker has made a film version of the book.

Angela's Ashes is the work of a mature man who has ruminated over his childhood in New York and Limerick for the best part of fifty years. It is a powerful, hard-hitting account which is impossible to ignore, whether you love it or hate its contents. The hunger, the cold, the smell of the chamber pots that are emptied in the latrines in the morning, the pain of growing up with an alcoholic father who rabbits on about dying for Ireland while neglecting his wife and children, all these are wonderfully captured through the memories of a perceptive child, who is recounting them in his sixties.

What is it about many Irish novelists that they need to leave their native land before writing about the experiences that happened to them there? (Joyce is the obvious example that comes to mind in this context.) According to Augustine Martin:

> For Joyce Ireland was among other things the old sow
> that ate her farrow; a country dedicated to the
> banishment of her artists.[1]

I don't presume to place Frank McCourt in the same literary category as Joyce, but this latest Irish literary talent shares with his illustrious predecessor a strong sentiment of exile. He was an outsider in New York because his parents were Irish, an exile on his return to Ireland because of his 'Yankee' accent and strange ways. More important than any geographical or sociological exile, however, is the feeling, so palpable in *Angela's Ashes*, of a spiritual, metaphysical malaise that convinces McCourt than he doesn't quite fit in anywhere. His parents were misfits, his brothers also, but none felt his marginality as strongly as the chronicler of his deprived youth who created, or recreated, *Angela's Ashes*. To my way of thinking, it doesn't matter much if all the events recounted in this book are true or not. What I felt after reading it was revulsion at the suffering endured by the McCourt family in the Limerick of the forties. The smell of the lanes, the black faces of the coal-man and the gasworks employees, the sinister and constant presence of the river Shannon and its perceived capacity to spread fever and death, the kindness and cruelty of the inhabitants of Limerick, were all vividly conveyed to me by the author. Despite my incredulity with regard to certain events (especially the feverish affair the narrator allegedly engages in with a consumptive young Protestant girl, or his 'warm' welcome to the shores of America by the lady from Poughkeepsie at the end of the book), which, in my opinion, smack of a desire to 'spice up' the narrative, I remain convinced of the overall validity of McCourt's testimony. After all, he is writing from memories of fifty to sixty years ago and such memories are bound to be unreliable in details. Such an approach leads to interesting reading as the imagination need not be curbed and the writer can be highly selective and choose material that suits the main thesis. It is fiction mingled with autobiography.

The theme of this chapter is the portrayal of the Catholic Church as an institution that was indifferent to the plight of the poor. McCourt's criticism is particularly virulent when he remembers how he never saw a priest darken the doorstep of his house, or that of any of the other houses in his area. Whereas nowadays the representatives of the Church are largely unwelcome in some of the poorer areas of our towns and cities, where religious practice is very low, in the 1940s they were still prestigious and influential – they would have been accorded respect anywhere, especially among the poor, who were very devout. The Catholic clergy rarely went hungry, unlike the vast bulk of their parishioners. But, in criticising the priests of the 1940s, is there not the risk of applying today's norms to a diametrically different situation? It was believed by many in Ireland in the 1940s that poverty was good for the soul, that all the pain you endured should be offered up to God on High. And then, of course, it has to be remembered that not all the representatives of the Church were self-centred, materialistic, full of their own importance. McCourt does describe, for example, the kindness of a Dominican priest, to whom he often went to confession:

> I wonder if the priest is asleep because he's very quiet till he says, My child, I sit here. I hear the sins of the poor. I assign the penance. I bestow absolution. I should be on my knees washing their feet. Do you understand me, my child?[2]

This was not the reaction of a worldly, functional priest. If anything, this particular Dominican has a strong Bernanosian quality, with the emphasis he places on the poor being the privileged ones in God's eyes. (That said, I doubt that any priest would express himself in these terms to a child.) I would prefer more balance in McCourt's portrayal of the Church. While I accept that there were several abuses among the Catholic clergy and the Christian Brothers during his childhood, I feel that he is most comfortable when highlighting defects, when describing the hopeless hardship and despair he and many like him had to endure, in part as a result of the Church's neglect. For while it certainly was a highly influential institution during the 1940s in Ireland, the Catholic Church could not be held responsible for all the inequality that existed in the period after Independence. The new Free State was too busy thinking about survival to set about eradicating hunger and injustice. Most of today's social services are provided by the State. In the forties and fifties, if the Church didn't run the schools and the orphanages, nobody else would have bothered to do so. It is natural that, now at the beginning of the third millennium, we feel horror at the conditions many people had to endure five decades ago. But let's not forget that in the 1940s, toilets, shoes, clothes, heat were luxuries that few could afford in adequate amounts. Sanitation as we know it was nowhere to be found. Small wonder then that so many people died of TB and typhoid: the miracle is that others survived at all. Poverty was the norm both in rural and urban families. The Depression, the Economic War and the Second World War ensured that was the case.

When reflecting on his past in Limerick, Frank McCourt's anti-clericalism is possibly the result of his disappointment at the Catholic Church's abandon, real or imaginary, of himself and his family. He might also be buying into the stereotypical vision of the Church as conceived by Joyce, a writer whose antipathy towards the said institution I have never properly understood. The opening page of *Angela's Ashes* announces the approach that will be adopted throughout:

> It was, of course, a miserable childhood: the happy childhood is hardly worth your while. Worse than the ordinary miserable childhood is the miserable Irish childhood, and worse yet is the miserable Irish Catholic childhood. (p. 1)

It cannot, and should not, be denied that McCourt was subjected to a great deal of trauma and humiliation during his childhood. He mentions 'the poverty; the shiftless loquacious alcoholic father; the pious defeated mother moaning by the fire; pompous priests; bullying schoolmasters; the English and the terrible things they did to us for 800 long years' (p. 1), as being the main sources of his unhappiness. Nevertheless, he does point out that, as a writer, this unhappy childhood has been worthwhile. You can't write well about experiences and feelings you've never lived through. McCourt is probably at his best when depicting black, hopeless situations, and in this the comparison with Dickens is probably apposite. The recapturing of his childhood nightmares in *Angela's Ashes*, the simplicity of the language, the child-like reactions to incomprehensible happenings, the humour, are all fine artistic achievements. I do not doubt McCourt's many literary talents, no more than I deny his right to portray the Catholic Church in a negative light, but I do at times call into question his objectivity and fairness. He captures wonderfully the groping middle-class shopkeepers who try to cheat the people who come to them with their Vincent de Paul food coupons – these same shopkeepers see themselves as upright, devout Catholics, the pillars of society. But he also evokes the fire and brimstone sermons given by the Redemptorist priests during retreats, the warmth of the churches compared to the harsh cold outside, the sweet smell of incense that permeated them. Strongest perhaps are the feelings of guilt and unworthiness that were instilled in people with regard to sexuality and the blind acceptance of dogmas that were handed down by well-fed priests in pulpits or in the schools. Religion recurs as a constant theme because of the dominant role it played in virtually everyone's life at the time. The clergy were so powerful largely because of the relative ignorance of the majority of the people when it came to philosophy or theology. The Irish diocesan clergy themselves were not exposed to a challenging training in these areas in the seminaries either. The people were happy to let the priests do their thinking for them and there weren't many who challenged the Church's line on anything. The following description of how the priest prepared the boys for their First Holy Communion is a classic of its type:

> He shows us how to stick out the tongue, receive the bit of paper, hold it a moment, draw in the tongue, fold your hands in prayer, look towards heaven, close your eyes in adoration, wait for the paper to melt in your mouth, swallow it, and thank God for the gift, the Sanctifying Grace wafting in on the odour of sanctity. (p. 134)

You can get a genuine glimpse into the child's reaction to this 'trial run' of his First Communion from these lines. The image of the 'Sanctifying Grace wafting in on the odour of sanctity' is quite special. First Communion and Confirmation were big events in the child's life and needed careful preparation.[3] It didn't matter either whether you were rich or poor, as these sacraments were available to all. Afterwards, despite the dire warnings from teachers, they all went off to collect money to mark the occasion. McCourt is even-handed in his depiction of these events. His hurt is obvious, however, when he writes about how he was refused permission by the sacristan to train to be an altar boy. His mother has no doubts as to the reasons for this rejection:

> They don't want boys from the lanes on the altar. They don't want the ones with scabby knees and hair sticking up. Oh no, they want the nice boys with hair oil and new shoes that have fathers with suits and ties and steady jobs. That's what it is and 'tis hard to hold on to the Faith with the snobbery that's in it. (p. 167)

What hits her even harder is the subsequent refusal by the Christian Brothers to allow her son to attend their secondary school, in spite of an excellent reference from his teacher in Leamy's (Primary School). (I have to say that this is extraordinary, and totally alien to the Christian Brothers' commitment to teaching the poor.) Angela comments on how this is the second time that the Church has slammed the door in her child's face. She has quite an ambivalent attitude to the Catholic Church. She possesses some of the resignation and piety that were widespread among Irish women of this period, but there are times when she rebels against the accepted norms. For example, when her husband suggests that it is her duty as a Catholic to submit to his sexual needs, she is heard to say: 'As long as there are no more children eternal damnation sounds attractive enough to me' (p. 246). This is a spirited reaction from a woman who should be the real focus of this book, were we to believe the title, that is. What she had to endure was undoubtedly more harrowing than the suffering of any of her offspring: the death of three of her children; her total neglect by her husband; the mortification she is subjected to by some representatives of the Vincent de Paul; her moral bankruptcy when she sleeps with Laman, in whose house they are forced to move after the father absconds to England and fails to send any money home. While the author has obvious sympathy for her plight, it didn't really suit his purposes in this book to confine himself to dealing with how this woman lived through such events and survived. His shock at seeing her begging in front of the church is, in his own words, 'the worst kind of shame' (p. 288). It is also clear that he feels great resentment towards her when he realises that she and Laman are 'at the excitement' (p. 340) in the loft of the house of the latter. At thirteen years of age, such revelations burn deeply into the psyche. In fairness to McCourt, he has mentioned in interviews that he needed to 'tell the full story' about his mother and the choices her life forced her into making. He was particularly shocked that his mother should have sex with Laman, but he also felt bitter at their father for leaving them, at society for placing them on the margins of civilised living, at the Catholic Church for abdicating its responsibility to the poor. All in all, he had a lot with which to reproach people and institutions. Mrs Spillane, an elderly woman to whom young Frank delivers telegrams, sums up the view of many people at the time when she says:

> There they are, the priests and nuns telling us Jesus was poor and 'tis no shame, lorries driving up to their houses with crates and barrels of whiskey and wine, eggs galore and legs of ham and they telling us what we should give up for Lent. Lent, my arse. What are we to give up when we have Lent all year long? (pp. 371-2)

How objective is this view, I wonder. Its validity is probably of limited relevance to this chapter. My thesis is that Frank McCourt has a relatively clichéd view of Ireland, one that has become firmly etched in many people's minds, that sees this island as an intellectually backward, unsavoury, depressing, priest-dominated, nostalgic country which constantly looks back bitterly on the pain inflicted on it by the English, and that blindly accepts the dictates of the Catholic Church. Part of the massive appeal of *Angela's Ashes* is probably a direct result of the surge of interest that has been generated this past decade around the globe, and especially in North America, with everything that has to do with Ireland and the Irish. McCourt, an Irish immigrant in America, was well-placed to write a memoir that would strike a cord with a wide audience. What was born out of his cathartic evocation of his childhood, *Angela's Ashes*, is a brutally frank and exquisitely written book. I don't necessarily find every single aspect of it fair or objective, but that doesn't prevent me from being awestruck at the power of some of his descriptions. When reading it, I experienced vicariously the hunger-pangs of the protagonists, their desolation and despair, their dignity sometimes in the face of adversity.

McCourt has achieved much fame and notoriety from *Angela's Ashes*, and deservedly so. However, I wonder to what extent his vision has been obscured by the years that have elapsed between when he lived through the experiences and when he finally got to put them in book form. Could it be – and I am only asking the question – that he has been unduly influenced in his portrayal of Irish society by James Joyce, for whom he admits a particular predilection? Augustine Martin noted in 1965 that for more than sixty years the Irish priest had been lambasted from every conceivable angle, and he warned:

> The artistic consciousness that accepts the formal and technical lessons of Joyce must be careful not to take over uncritically Joyce's fierce irrational anti-clericalism.[4]

McCourt, too, is fiercely anti-clergy. He would have done well to heed Martin's warning. He dwells very much on the negative aspects of religion, on the authoritarian and worldly priests who were at variance with the Gospel's message of humility and poverty. I don't subscribe a conscious desire on his part to describe events in a different light to the reality of the time. But not everyone from a poor background had a similar experience of the Church. One has only to consider Críostóir O'Flynn's account of his childhood to realise that there are two views of such poverty. O'Flynn is on record as saying that he found McCourt's depiction of Limerick unbalanced. His own memoir is probably a more accurate, even if far less compelling, chronicle of the Limerick of their youth. However, the laboured description of the problems surrounding his baptism and some of his schooling do not hold the reader's attention nearly as well as McCourt's pathos and drama. There is no doubt as to which is the better read. O'Flynn has many reservations about the religious instruction he was given and the hardship he had to endure, but at no stage does he slip into the facile tendency to taint everyone for the sins of the few. Throughout his life, he has maintained certain religious beliefs, as he himself explains:

> I too have kept the faith – thanks to the mercy of God, to the prayers of my mother and others, and to the example of many good Catholics, priests and religious and lay people, I have known from my childhood to the present day. As I compare the Ireland we grew up in to the Ireland of today, I am mystified by the fact that so many people nowadays give up the practice of the Catholic religion, while others want to pick and choose the doctrines they will accept or reject.[5]

O'Flynn's dealings with priests and religious were more positive than those of McCourt. He is also very good at highlighting the negative impact that rampant secularisation has had on this country in between. Because of the scandals within the Church and our improved economic performance in recent years, religious practice has been relegated to a minor preoccupation in the minds of many. O'Flynn points out that their Divine Founder told the apostles that there would always be scandals. Because a few people don't live up to acceptable Christian norms does not of itself mean that the underlying tenets of religion should automatically be abandoned. (Remember Peter's oaths of non-recognition of his leader and the scattering of the chosen few.) There is much worship of the God of Mammon in the Ireland of today, and this has led to a spiritual void in modern society. Money of itself cannot lead to happiness or fulfilment. There is also a need, according to O'Flynn, for a more objective evaluation of the contribution of the religious to the education of the young for many decades:

> ...they were people who had given up everything for the love of God so that they could help others. And even though some of them were too fond of beating us with leather or stick, ...they all worked very hard, not to get anything for themselves, like the people in business or the politicians, but to help the likes of us to get on in life and to live in a way that would help us to get to heaven when we died.[6]

How many of the children of the thirties, forties and fifties would have had a chance of second-level education but for the Christian Brothers and the Mercy nuns. This short parenthesis is not an effort to undermine McCourt's description of his childhood, but rather to show that another equally valid view exists, expressed by a fellow Limerickman of the same period, who was also poor and underprivileged. For the moment, let us conclude with McCourt. My worry was that the positive aspects of the wonderful *Angela's Ashes* might be ruined by a sensational and exaggerated sequel. I feared this because of my unease at the last pages of the book, which added nothing to the overall effect. The story should logically have concluded when the hero boarded the ship for America. That was the end of his childhood in Ireland and the beginning of another story. That story has now been told in the recently published sequel – *'Tis*, which, though not sensational or exaggerated, has not enjoyed anything like the response to *Angela's Ashes*. Not surprising, given that this memoir of his childhood is a classic of its type.

NOTES

1. Augustine Martin, 'Inherited Dissent: the Dilemma of the Irish Writer', *Studies*, Spring 1965, p. 1.
2. *Angela's Ashes* (Flamingo, 1997), p. 208.
3. Christóir O'Flynn, *There is an Isle: a Limerick Boyhood Childhood* (Cork: Mercier Press, 1998), did not portray his childhood in Limerick during this period in the same way as McCourt (we will discuss this later in this chapter) but he does have similar memories of the sacraments: 'There was too much tension associated with all the preparation for our first Confession and the practising for the reception of Holy Communion, learning the hymns, being drilled in what to do with your tongue and your teeth' (p. 186).
4. 'Inherited Dissent', op. cit., p. 15.
5. *There is an Isle*, op. cit., pp. 269-70.
6. Ibid., p. 348.